# DUSTY LAND

## STORIES OF TWO TEACHERS IN THE KALAHARI

Also by John Ashford

*Meeting the Mantis —*
*Searching for a Man in the Desert*
*and Finding the Kalahari Bushmen*

Peace Corps Writers, 2015

# DUSTY LAND

## STORIES OF TWO TEACHERS IN THE KALAHARI

JOHN ASHFORD

A PEACE CORPS WRITERS BOOK

DUSTY LAND —
STORIES OF TWO TEACHERS IN THE KALAHARI

A Peace Corps Writers Book — an imprint of Peace Corps Worldwide

Copyright © 2017 by John Ashford

Printed in the United States of America

by Peace Corps Writers of Oakland, California.

"Topo" appeared in the *Silk Road Review,* vol. 6, no. 2.

"Boycott" appeared in *One by One: Thirty-One Years of the Peace Corps in Botswana* (1997)

For more information, contact peacecorpsworldwide@gmail.com.

Peace Corps Writers and the Peace Corps Writers colophon are trademarks of PeaceCorpsWorldwide.org

ISBN-13: 978-1-935925-88-0

Library of Congress Control Number: 2017954249

First Peace Corps Writers Edition, December, 2017

# STORIES

# Introduction

IN OUR MIDDLE AGE and in the middle of our careers, my wife Genevieve and I joined the Peace Corps to create a change in the rhythm of our lives. I had worked in one school or another for about thirty years, and it was no secret that I was getting a bit dry, and was ready for a change. We had been together for about five years, and though we hadn't gotten married yet, we had purchased a house together — a fixer-upper, and I was doing a lot of fixing up on evenings and weekends.

For many years I had nursed a yearning to go into the Peace Corps, but Gen still enjoyed doing what she was doing — selling real estate, and she had some reservations about moving to a foreign country. So we made the decision to try working overseas for a summer. I built a storage room in our basement to cache our belongings, and we rented out our house, hired a manager, and moved, first to Bangkok, Thailand, and then back to Seattle with plans to apply to become Peace Corps Volunteers.

In Seattle we spent our time house sitting. We got married. We stayed in touch with the Peace Corps. We accepted an invitation to serve as Volunteers in Botswana.

In mid-November of 1990 we flew to Chicago for an orientation, then on to the Gaborone to begin our training. In January 1991 Gen and I were sworn in as "PCVs."

THE STORIES IN THIS COLLECTION represent the two years that Gen and I spent in the Peace Corps in Botswana. I've tried to show some of the pleasures, responsibilities, enjoyment, and strains of serving in a developing country.

The early stories like "At the Pond" and "Talk Like a Man" are from the training period that lasted from late November, when we arrived in Botswana, to the following January, when we graduated from training.

My assignment was to lecture at the Tonota College of Education, a new teacher training college, but when we arrived at the village, the second year students I was supposed to teach were doing their practice teaching in various parts of the country so I taught English at a secondary school nearby. Gen was assigned to teach home-ec at a school eight kilometers away. Stories in the collection from that period include "Unhinged (Temporarily)," "Tim and the Five Paragraph Essay," and "Diamonds."

Teaching at the college yielded several stories that include "Outsider," "Sacrificial Beasts," "The Dean's Garden," "Boycott," and "Staff Tea."

There are several stories that don't fit any of the categories above. The story "Topo," for instance. I got to know a young man named Topo when I taught at the secondary school, but the story takes place long after I left the school when I had a chance meeting with him on the road where I was taking an afternoon walk.

"Beginner's Mind" is a story that takes place several months before we entered the Peace Corps, during a time when I was trying to organize a job overseas for the two of us as a part of my effort to convince Gen that living overseas would work. In contrast, "On Safari" takes place ten years after we left the Peace Corps, at a time when Gen and I returned as tourists traveling in southern Africa. "Lunch in Lusaka" also takes place after we left Botswana, as we traveled to Dar-es-Salaam and were trying to get our visas in order so that we could enter Tanzania and Kenya.

I was touched by a number of people I met or worked with in Botswana. The family I stayed with during the part of training called "village-live-in" started me acquiring the language. I never really became fluent, but thanks to them I spoke enough Setswana that Gen and I could function in parts of the country where we didn't meet anyone who spoke English. Molifi, the young man I met in the story, "At the Pond," showed me the vast gulf that existed between my expectations and the reality of many people's lives in the country.

The lives of people in a Third World country are often very difficult. They grow up with few material objects and I've tried to show that in "Diamonds," "Topo," and other stories.

Often, out of conflict or in the midst of tensions that apparently have no way of getting resolved, a wonderful experience blossoms. In the story of "Boycott," for instance, I felt like I was being hounded, but suddenly came to an insight that turned everything around. A similar experience takes place in the "Feast of Krishna."

My hope is that as you, the reader, go through the stories in this collection, you will begin to have a vicarious experience of what it is like to serve in Africa in the Peace Corps.

# DUSTY LAND

STORIES OF TWO TEACHERS IN THE KALAHARI

**SUMMER 1990**

## Beginner's Mind

MY FLIGHT LEFT BOMBAY at 3:00 a.m. It stopped twice, in Delhi and Calcutta, and at four in the afternoon landed in Bangkok. As I left the aircraft, every sense in my body was on edge. Traveling internationally was new for me.

Entering the steamy heat I was wearing headphones with the wry-sweet sound of Paul Desmond on alto sax playing "Glad to be Unhappy." I listened to the album frequently, and the mellow sound soothed my mood whenever I was in an anxious state, as I certainly was that day — I had a week in Thailand to find jobs for Gen and me.

Along with 450 other passengers crowded four- or five-abreast, I shuffled slowly down a gray-carpeted floor enclosed in a long tube. My first journey away from North America and I was shoulder to shoulder in a sea of fellow travelers, pushed along haltingly by invisible forces into the Don Muang International Airport terminal. We were jostling, bumping into carry-on luggage, hoping to be on our way toward customs.

Judging from appearances, most of my fellow passengers were Asian or Middle Eastern, and based on the style of their luggage and the way some of the people clung to each other, I guessed that many of my travel companions on the ramp appeared to be refugees from regions where a war was heating up or where terrorist activities made life unbearable.

I was a refugee from burnout and the wars I faced were all internal.

THIRTY YEARS EARLIER, I'd gone to work in a school because I loved teaching. I liked the contact with students. I loved it when they came to my classroom after school to tell me about their lives. I enjoyed it when a high school kid brought in a guitar or 5-string banjo and we got together in an office or conference room to practice picking out tunes. In those days I was passionate about hikes with the Outdoor Club, and the adventure of camping in the snow with a group of goofy teens.

For about ten years I did those things, then a job in administration came along and I moved to a community college. Twenty years later, as far as students were concerned, I was a suit. Instead of driving a beat-up VW bug and feeling invigorated by my work, I drove a Volvo and felt worn down by administrative responsibilities. Only a few embers of enthusiasm remained — barely any glow at all, hardly any heat.

It wasn't exactly a consolation that I remembered my father going through the same type of experience. He fumed for years about a job that he found unsatisfying and finally his reward was a diagnosis of a fatal illness. For years, I'd been grousing and complaining internally about my work until I began to hear echoes of my father's frustration. It felt as if I had carried his dissatisfaction into my middle age. I'd seen him die at the age of forty-six and as I passed through my forties and into my early fifties, I was doubly aware that every year I gained in age was possibly borrowed time.

I received hints from Gen, as well.

She and I had been living together for only a short time and more than once she told me, "It's like you drop into a cave and disappear

4

during the day. I never hear about what you've done or where you've been. You never talk about your work."

Her comments stung and made me aware that when I came home from work, what I really wanted was to erase the memory of that day. Eventually, I came to realize that I needed to return my life to a focus on things that gave me energy and purpose.

At first, I just didn't know how. After working at the same job too long, I'd forgotten what those things were. Intellectually, I knew that life would feel fresh if only I could encounter something new in my day. But living in a state of burnout, it was difficult to feel as if I was learning anything new.

I had a shift in my outlook when more and more refugees began to attend the college, and I started to meet them. They were from all over the world, particularly Southeast Asia.

I got to know some of them well enough that I felt compassion for what they'd been through. Their experiences as immigrants didn't match the patriotic myth about happy newcomers arriving on our shore. Every one of them had left the certainties of a place they knew quite well. Most of them arrived confused with very little in the way of material wealth. What they had were their customs, their language, and their family, often under assault in the new environment. They'd all been through a journey, made several stops along the way, and overcome many obstacles. By the time they reached their destination, most were in mourning for the loss of friendships and close relatives.

AS WE PASSENGERS CONTINUED through the tunnel it made an accordion bend and I was pushed through the turn into a hallway. Movement of the crowd slowed, and I was forced to move with short little steps.

I began to remember a Vietnamese student named Thieu, a young man who could barely speak English when I first met him. He had shown up in my office one afternoon with a newspaper clipping.

"Help me?" he asked in his rudimentary English. "Want read this."

The article was one he'd clipped from the Seattle newspaper the previous day and the subject was the collapse of the Berlin Wall. Although he understood the gist of it — that people were getting their freedom — he wanted to make sure he understood the details. We spent an hour translating the article into words he could understand, and he told me about his life.

Thieu had been drafted into the North Vietnamese army.

"At seventeen," he told me, "I was a communist soldier."

He managed to crawl through a sewer, escape, and make his way across Laos to a refugee camp in Thailand.

Helping Thieu with English, I latched onto language as the key to bringing change in my life. I already had college degrees, but after meeting Thieu, I entered a program at the university to be certified in a new career as an ESL teacher.

Now making my way into the airport, I hoped my new skills would be a ticket to finding work in Thailand.

The throng of passengers ahead of me began to thin and I entered a low-ceilinged, shadowy corridor. The only light in the passage came from several office windows along one wall. A uniformed man directed traffic here and some people — those who required a visa to enter the country — were directed to one of the office windows. I flashed my American passport and was sent directly to customs. My feeling at that moment — accepting it as my right, it was only natural that I'd bypass red tape and be sent to the head of the line. I fully expected preferential treatment.

I had my passport stamped, and, after riding down a long escalator, headed into the main concourse to pick up my luggage. In the huge hall, distances seemed inexhaustible. I tried reading signs, but many of them were written in a totally unintelligible script.

In what seemed an endless walk through the concourse, I thought about how I had wished for this change. A voice in my head kept teasing, *Be careful what you wish for.* Everywhere, I saw reminders that I had made a shift away from a familiar environment. I was a beginner here and I quickly realized that preferential treatment was over. Kaput!

On my way to the baggage carousel I made an effort to study the geography of the place in order to memorize the layout. I'd be back here in one week to fly home to Seattle. My duffel, containing my belongings for the first leg of my journey, was waiting on the carousel. I didn't need it in Thailand, so I took it directly to the "Left Bags" window to check it for seven days. I walked away with only my carry-on bag so I could travel light.

At the far end of the airport building a billboard-sized photograph covering an entire wall with the face of Mel Gibson advertised the American cop movie *Lethal Weapon*. Underneath the sign, a number of coffee shop tables and chairs were clustered in a corner near a souvenir shop. I headed in that direction. It looked like a place I could sit and get my bearings.

CHANGING MY LIFESTYLE had become an obsession for me, and for two years after I became involved with ESL teaching, Gen and I talked about making changes. I needed more than just a move from one job to another. I wanted something more meaningful. I wanted to live overseas.

"What about disease?" Gen asked. "How will we stay healthy?"

Also, she was in the position of having to give up a career she enjoyed.

"The other thing," she said to me, "is that I don't want to sit around. There has to be some kind of job for me. Maybe I'm not a teacher, but I want to do something."

The whole idea made Gen nervous, but she was willing to explore the possibilities.

The process began with me applying for a teacher exchange in China. But a few months after I applied, Tiananmen Square was in the news and returning teachers told me that the climate there had changed — Chinese students were extremely nervous about dealing with Western teachers. After that, I took Gen to an informational meeting about the Peace Corps.

Then, I gave notice at work that I was going to leave.

My job had ended one month before I entered the Bangkok airport. Everything I'd done in the previous two years had led up to this moment. My arrival in Bangkok was right on schedule.

ON MY WAY TO THAILAND, I spent three weeks in an ashram in India where my son was living. I'd gone there mainly to visit him, but it also seemed like a place to start, a way of jolting me out of old work habits and routines, of reconnecting with parts of myself I'd lost touch with.

I attended several lectures at the ashram, and in one, a woman swami dressed in orange robes spoke Hindi while a young Western woman translated into English. "You are not your body," she said. "Imagine your body as a column of light. Your thoughts are light. Your feelings are light. You are light."

At the time, the words of the swami seemed ambiguous and I puzzled about the meaning. Perhaps it was another way of saying *it's all illusion*. Or, it might have been a way of thinking that there is more than one reality. I tried seeing the world in the way that she suggested. First I imagined pointing a flashlight beam in different directions, then that my mind was a column of light. Finally I began to think that I'd never understand the kind of experience she was suggesting.

There were hundreds of people at the ashram, and in the dining hall there were about fifty tables arranged on a huge marble floor.

One evening, I sat down at a table with four strangers. How I happened to pick this table was pure chance. Carrying a dinner tray with both hands, I saw an empty chair, gave a silent nod to one of the people — a request, *May I join your group?* She responded in the affirmative by extending a hand toward the vacant chair.

By way of introducing myself, I told them I was on my way to Thailand to look for a teaching job. To my surprise, all four of the people worked in Thailand. They were taking a short break from their teaching jobs. They all knew the territory. Was this a confirmation I was doing the right thing? That's the way I took it at the time. All of them knew people there and gave me names. They even recommended a guesthouse in Bangkok as a place to stay.

The conversation put me into a whirlwind of details and note-taking — and excitement.

BEFORE FINDING SEATING in the airport, I bought a map of the city in the souvenir shop. I then sat down at a small table in the café, pulled out my notes from that chance meeting at the ashram from my small carry-on bag, and began locating some of the places recommended by my new acquaintances. Finding my direction had been a major part of my focus during these two years of obsession. I pored over the map like a man who'd lost his way, trying to get back on course.

The whole time in the airport I thought about my obsession, my focus on this one direction. I thought about how things had changed already. Holding a job for twenty years, leading a life that held few surprises, I'd gotten used to waking up in the morning expecting another predictable day. Thanks to this obsession, here I was in a foreign airport confronted with change and unpredictability everywhere. Printed signs I couldn't read, announcements over the P.A. I couldn't understand. There were not many familiar touch points, but the voice inside kept at me. *This is what you wanted.*

Leaving the airport terminal, I flagged down a small, three-wheeled, motorized vehicle called a *tuk-tuk* to find the guesthouse I'd located on the map — it was a fair distance from the airport.

Along the way, we passed sidewalk vendors cooking spicy foods and I became familiar with the smell of Bangkok. Spices mingling with the fumes of traffic — black smoke from diesel buses, blue gaseous vapors from tuk-tuks and motorcycles. As we entered the central part of the city, we passed an elephant carrying a load of furniture, a man walking by his side along the busy thoroughfare. A sure sign I was no longer in Seattle.

I didn't realize until the next day that the neighborhood surrounding the guesthouse was not a particularly tourist-friendly area. In the morning I was shooed out of a tea shop. I had already taken a seat at a small table, but when the owner saw me, there was no mistaking the fact that he didn't want to serve *farangs* (foreigners). Although he didn't have any customers at the time, he waved his hands, speaking in Thai. The only English he knew was, "No-no-no."

I went to another restaurant where I was also evicted. Not as vehemently, but they wouldn't serve anyone who couldn't read the menu. That was my impression anyway — no one said it in English.

I made an appointment on the telephone for an interview for a job, and found the area where the office was located — in a narrow *soi* (driveway) — near the center of the city. I had thirty minutes before the one o'clock meeting, and I still hadn't eaten a thing.

I wandered the street hungry and thirsty. Finally I sat on a curb to rest. Soon I spotted a man riding past on a bicycle. On the back of his bike he had a glass steam box and inside I saw Chinese-style dumplings!

I called out to the man, *"hum-bao!"* — the name of my favorite style of Chinese dumpling. I'd learned about it in Seattle's International District. No sooner had I spoken, than an astonishing thing happened — the man understood me. He stopped immediately, propped up his bike, and, smiling the whole time, pulled a dumpling from his box. He even had a Thermos of green tea. I was grateful, as if he had saved my life.

That first morning in Bangkok I learned to enjoy my status as a beginner. I didn't know a word of Thai and no one I had met spoke English. I was dealing with a totally new world. But my mind was working and I was alert.

I went to the headquarters for refugee camps to interview for a job; the man I spoke with — in English, of course — suggested that I go to their office in a village called Phanat Nikhom, introduce myself, and let them know that I was interested in working in a camp.

The village of Phanat Nikhom was near a refugee camp where many of my students in Seattle had been processed. Fortunately for me, there was a demand for English-speaking teachers.

When I left the interview, I again thought of the Vietnamese man named Thieu. *Isn't it ironic? I am also going to a refugee camp in Thailand to look for freedom.* It was obviously a different kind of freedom, but the parallel was striking.

The village was about 30 miles south of Bangkok, and I had to take a bus. At a ticket window I said, "Phanat Nikhom" and slid my money across the counter. The ticket seller counted it out, then passed back a ticket and change. At the bus lot a dozen buses nosed into the curb, all identified by signs written in Thai script. Using gestures and hand pointing, I asked for help finding the right bus. I boarded the bus and remained alert to where I was supposed to get off, since the bus made a loop through several villages and I couldn't tell one from the other.

As I traveled to the village, I was navigating a new reality. Everything I did that day called for me to be a beginner. Everywhere I went, I got reminders that in Thailand, I was illiterate. Remembering the words of the swami in India, I tried out the idea of shining a flashlight on my feelings. With every new experience I tried seeing things in a new way. There was nothing I could do without help. Sometimes, when I asked for help I couldn't understand the response. I had to rely on skills I didn't know I possessed and invent ways to get where I had to go.

At Phanat Nikhom we were hired, all we had to do was show up in July. The offer was for summer jobs for both Gen and me. We'd be working at the refugee camp for a consortium of three agencies: Save the Children, World Education, and Experiment in International

11

Living. We'd have a chance to try life overseas and, hopefully, to find a way of responding to Gen's reservations about staying healthy.

I returned to Bangkok that same day just in time to catch an overnight train north to the city of Chiang Mai to see its more than three hundred Buddhist temples. This was a place I had always wanted to visit.

Vendors there sold food on the street, and all I had to do was point in order to get a delicious meal. But I became overcome with the heat and had to find something to drink. I went to a covered, outdoor stand where produce was sold. Papayas, mangoes, and other tropical fruit covered a counter that was shaded by a broad tent with a green-fringed awning. I could see that there was a large cooler on the other side of the counter. It was plugged into a generator and in the cooler I saw bottles of soft drinks. The labels on the bottles all said "Green Spot."

A woman was standing behind boxes of produce, and when I got her attention, I said to her, pronouncing the name as carefully as I could, "Green Spot." I leaned toward her and felt a certainty: the way to make myself understood was to say the word with the best unaccented American pronunciation I could muster. Very carefully, I emphasized the American "r" and each consonant as I would with my ESL students. But when she looked at me with a puzzled expression, all I could do was repeat myself. The woman began to fidget impatiently. I understood her body language perfectly well, because I was slightly frustrated myself.

But I was dying of thirst, and finally I had a burst of inspiration. It took an act of re-imagining the word itself. *I had to shine a light on it and try to see it in a new way.* In an ESL class in Seattle, American pronunciation was the model students were to strive for. But as I began to understand, I was in Thailand, facing a new situation entirely. People here could care less about American pronunciation. So, I pronounced the name, Green Spot, the way I imagined an Asian in one of my classes might say the word, "Ga-rain-a Sa-pot-a."

Without another word, the woman turned and pulled a bottle from the cooler. She opened it and gave me a straw. I paid and took a sip of my cool soda pop. The icy moisture from the side of the bottle dripped satisfyingly through my fingers as I walked away.

The entire transaction had taken less than a minute. A small thing, but a beginning.

# NOVEMBER 1990

to

# JANUARY 1991

## Talk Like A Man

I HELD MY RED DUFFEL BAG by the handle and stood there feeling awkward. I'd been in Africa for ten days and now had come to live with an African family, but I had no idea what to expect.

Mma Letlape was sitting in the middle of her yard awaiting my arrival. She was wearing a blue sarong with a flowered blouse, and was surrounded by a group of adolescents and children who had gathered to see my van drive up to her yard. On her lap she was holding a crying infant. I realized that it was in some kind of pain as she daubed its hand with the thick stub of a broken aloe vera leaf. (Later I learned that the baby had crawled into a cooking fire.)

Mma looked at me and right away she began to laugh at the idea of having a white-skinned, middle-aged man coming to live in her house.

"*Dumela* (Hello)," I said. It was one of the few Setswana words I knew at that point.

IN ORDER FOR ME to become acquainted with the culture of Botswana and begin to learn the some of its language, I would be a part of this household for almost two weeks. I was in the phase of Peace Corps training called the "Village Live-In."

Mma immediately began doing her part with my language training. As she held the infant tenderly on her lap, she began telling everyone in the yard, "*Bua Setswana fela*. (Speak Setswana only.)" Spreading aloe vera gel like butter on the baby's hand, she repeated the rule for me and everyone else. Her children and grandchildren had learned some English in school, but they were not to use it around me and she made it very clear to me that I was to toe the line — learning the language was my job, it was not an option.

Having been jostled in the back seat of the van for hours, I felt disoriented, but during the previous days, one of our trainers had told me, "You won't be recognized as a man until you speak their language." Learning a new language, I hoped, could be a start in my loosening up.

In preparation for this experience, the trainers told our group, "You'll be part of the family. The parents will be your parents. As long as you're in their home, you'll be considered a son or daughter." I hardly knew what they meant.

I was in my mid-fifties and it had been forty years since my father died. I hadn't lived with a parent since my late teens. The idea of living with a family appealed to me, and it seemed like an excellent way to learn the language and the culture, but the notion that I'd be a son, that someone would be my parent, was more than I could comprehend. When I tried to picture how it might go, all I could conjure up was a sense of confusion — an uncomfortable stirring began in my stomach. I was very much aware of my anxiety as I stood in the yard surveying the scene with Mma and the crowd of young people.

MMA'S FULL NAME was Keitumetse Letlape. (The name she was addressed by was pronounced mmmm-mă'). She was a sixty-six-year-old woman, and a whirlwind of energy with skin the color of light coffee. Her round face could move from welcoming to happiness to extreme irritation in an instant. But I learned right away, she was the mother and she made the rules. As far as she was concerned, in the household hierarchy, I was just another one of the children.

Gen was staying in a household a quarter of a mile away. We had asked to stay in separate houses so we'd both learn as much as possible. Every morning I walked to her house and, together, we went to a classroom to study Setswana grammar. Midday, when I returned home, Mma fixed tea. We sat at a table made of coarsely milled lumber. The table sagged in the middle because it lacked glue in the cross-supports underneath. After taking her snuff, Mma began pointing to household objects and drilling the names into my head. She'd ask a question, then shout at me, bully me, until I understood. Usually she helped me answer, but her persistence was limitless. By dinnertime, I had a headache.

Within the family, even the youngest members knew how to speak. Of course, they had grown up speaking the language. They found it hilarious that a grown man couldn't speak properly. When guests dropped by, the main topic of conversation was the *makoa* (the white man) who didn't know how to speak. Everyone laughed and made fun of my attempts. I spent a lot of time that week feeling isolated. But in the evening, five children crowded around my bed and we made up conversations. As a starting point, I drew pictures on a blank page in my journal. The children ranged in age from five to sixteen, and in those moments, I began to feel the warmth of being part of the family.

Sometimes Mma felt it necessary to give me lessons in behavior.

We sat outside to eat our midday meal and one afternoon after I finished lunch I didn't know what to do with my enameled metal bowl. The dishwater and soap were in a plastic tub on a board near the cooking area. I walked over to the tub and scrubbed and rinsed my bowl.

The family was appalled.

The older sons laughed with embarrassment. Mma and her daughter were aghast. Mma made a sarcastic remark that didn't need translation. But by that time, I was accustomed to being the buffoon. Later, Mma told me in no uncertain terms, a man does not cook and he does not wash dishes. Her thirty-year old daughter, Butsile, was responsible for household chores and any request had to be made to her.

Butsile was unmarried and had four children. I never did learn the circumstances of her life, but guessed that her fiancé worked in the mines in South Africa as did many of the men of the village. Marriage customs in Botswana don't frown on having children before marriage, but before a couple can have their union recognized, the man must pay the "bride price," amounting to the cost of several cattle. In village society, marriage is one of the tasks of a man's life. Until he completes it, he's treated like a young boy. Often it takes years to save the money.

I DID MY BEST to fit in with the routines in the home, but after three days I hadn't figured out how to get a bath. Water was extremely scarce, but a bath becomes a necessity. I practiced phrases, tried to get my vocabulary together, and in the late afternoon approached Butsile, keeper of the bath water. First, she laughed, then her eyes darted from side to side. She was confused. It took a few minutes before she understood. Her confusion was my fault. I'd used the word for "washing clothes" and she thought I wanted her to do my laundry. I had to act out my request to make her understand, "I want to wash my body."

After dinner, Butsile began making preparations. She brought grass mats and goat skins into the hallway room by my bed. She hung a blanket over the door and I heard her telling the younger children not to bother me. Then she brought in a large galvanized tub — in the U.S. I'd seen tubs like that being used as funky double basses by string bands.

Butsile thumped the tub. *"Bata,"* she said. In a few minutes she returned with a large steaming kettle. Pouring almost an inch of hot water into the tub, she left me to my luxury.

MY HOST FATHER, the man of the house, was Rra (mister [r·ră]) Letlape. He and I didn't have a chance to introduce ourselves the afternoon I arrived. That day he lay in the shade of his house wrapped in a plaid wool blanket, coughing into a bloody bandana. The sound of his coughing awakened something deep in my memory. I heard a particular kind of fatigue: the coughing of one who has taken about all they can withstand. When I was young, my father's cough sounded like that in the weeks before he died. I hadn't thought about my father for years and the awareness startled me.

Letlape was at his best in the morning when he felt rested. I'd been in the home for a few days when he invited me to sit outside with him for morning tea. We tilted our hard wooden chairs, leaning the backs against the blue wall of the house while Butsile hurried past doing her chores, her freshly laundered skirt brushing the ground, her hair wrapped neatly with a blue bandana. The sunlight had barely begun to filter through flat-topped acacias at the top of a nearby cliff, but already she had swept the hard surface of the dirt patio, her stiff-bristled broom leaving a regular pattern of geometric arcs in the sand.

Gusts of wind rattled the corrugated metal roof behind us as we watched birds flying overhead. Storks circled high above and a few clouds hung in the sky. I wanted to ask Letlape how his trip to the clinic had gone the day before, but I didn't have the language. He and Mma had left before sunrise to catch the bus into town. They returned after I'd gone to bed.

Since he'd invited me to sit with him that morning, it didn't seem to matter that our conversation was limited. Letlape's wrinkled, intelligent face was a marvel to watch as he seemed to make calculations and plans. He said something to me that I didn't understand, but

I had the impression he wanted to teach me something about subsistence farming. He seemed to use every sense, his black leathery face getting the scent of the wind, feeling the temperature, gauging the direction of the clouds. He talked about it all as fast as he could. Then, he seemed to become agitated, as if he was eager to tell me something more.

Although she was busy, his daughter paid us solicitous attention. She seemed to enjoy the fact that we sat together in the swept yard. Even as she scurried to feed the household and get small children off to school, Butsile sent her younger sister to the *kraal* (fenced enclosure), where the goats were kept, for a cup of milk. She scalded the goat milk over the fire and poured it into our tea. I held the enameled metal cup between my fingers for the warmth and listened to Letlape. Butsile spoke a limited amount of English and as she hurried past on her way to the kitchen, she stopped to translate, "He wants to tell you storks bring rain."

Letlape wore a long wool coat, its hem badly tattered, and I imagined it might be a relic of World War II. On a wall inside the house, I'd looked at photographs of him wearing a British army uniform taken during the war. But because of my lack of language, I had no way to ask about his wartime experience.

For a few minutes, we all sat in silence and the storks circled lower and lower.

Letlape rolled a cigarette using his knee as a kind of table; then he smoked and sipped his tea. When he started to talk again, I couldn't understand, but he became emphatic and I sensed his frustration. It seemed urgent, as if there was something I had to know.

Finally, fishing through deep coat pockets, he produced a small bottle. "*Dipilisi*," he repeated several times until I realized he was trying to teach me the word.

"Ahh, dipilisi — pills," I said.

Butsile was a few feet away stirring sour sorghum porridge. "The pills," she said, "they are going to make him well." She said the words like a prayer. "He's going to get well," she said, pointing to the directions typed in English on the label, a covenant that seemed to guarantee a miracle.

She handed me the cylindrical container and I looked at the label. Take two pills four times a day. On a separate line it read, "Acetaminophen" — the generic name for Tylenol.

The clinic had not exactly prescribed a wonder drug, but Butsile, with a gesture full of conviction, put down her pan and pointed again to the label. Proudly, her eyes brimming, "He is going to get well," she repeated.

I nodded and said, *"Go siame."* (Very good.) I remembered when my father was dying and everyone tried to find cause for hope.

That afternoon as Letlape had predicted, it rained hard for an hour and the family crowded close inside the hut watching the downpour. Goats left the kraal to huddle under the dripping corrugated metal eaves. Some even tried to enter the house.

After the rain stopped, the muddy ground was covered with the wings of termites. Also, pink fuzzy insects crawled on the sand and flocks of small birds swooped in to gorge themselves. In the field beyond, stiff legged on the red earth, storks plucked up tender frogs struggling to emerge from their long hibernation.

Normally, I'm fascinated watching birds. But on that day, standing in the doorway behind Letlape, aware of steam rising from his shoulders, what I saw was a very thin line between life and death, survival and extinction.

I didn't have to ask about anything.

THAT NIGHT MONTSHO, the family's thirty-seven-year-old son — and my roommate, returned from a bar in the village eager to talk. As his lilting baritone droned, our small room became filled with his beery breath. I dozed off, and woke myself up with a snore, then couldn't get back to sleep. I lay in the narrow bed with the image in my mind of the small cot where my father lay when he was dying.

In my half-sleep, I began to think I was in that other bed. The image became a nightmare and repeated itself over and over. It circulated through my mind all night. Sometimes it was me in the small bed. At other times, I saw my father wrapped in his sheet, the way he looked when I came home from school the day he died.

WHENEVER THERE WERE EVENTS, Mma took me along. Her husband was too sick to attend and she felt it was her responsibility to take me.

For those occasions — village meetings or funerals — Mma wore a flowered wrap-around skirt, a yellow blouse, and a blue bandana tied in her hair. I never knew where we were going. She tried to explain with much gesturing and shouting, but I was never sure what she was talking about. After we arrived at these events, I sat with her in a circle of village women.

Normally, the men segregated themselves, but I'll never know what the men talked about at these gatherings. As I sat among the women, I became the main topic of their conversation. They wanted to know about me. *How did this white man get here? Do you really think he's intelligent? Will he ever learn to speak with adults?* Mma Letlape handled the situation with dignity, although I'm sure she was as uncomfortable as I was.

I felt like a cuckoo hatchling in a foreign nest. I was taller than everyone else. I might have emerged from a speckled egg deposited by stealth to be raised by a family of domestic sparrows.

The feeling was familiar. It was the way I'd felt as an awkward adolescent when I was stranded in the company of adults. I found myself revisiting my life at age fourteen — the worst period of my life and a time I'd tried for years to block and obliterate from my memory.

At that age, I learned to drive without my parents' knowledge — it was my way of declaring independence. When my parents found out, I was in deep trouble, of course. But my father could no longer drive and my mother had never learned. And so, though I was much too young for a license, I became the driver for the family.

They needed transportation to take my father to his doctor's appointments. My mother was beginning a new career — she'd gotten a job at the University — and she sometimes needed a ride to work or to social events related to her work.

The social events were the worst part. For me, these often led to my being the only adolescent in a roomful of adults. My mouth became dry. I felt clumsy and speechless. Forty years later, here I was, attending "adult" social occasions with Mma Letlape and feeling, again, as I had at fourteen.

It seems that I had come to this village still carrying the experience of loss and voiceless confusion from my youth. As I allowed these unresolved emotions to rise to the surface, I remembered how difficult that time of my life was — for me and for the family. The father nearing death. The family preparing for his departure. Household conversation centering on news of his gains or setbacks. The mother making preparations to be on her own and bearing her grief in silence because open expression would be premature.

I didn't need to be fluent in Setswana to understand the dynamics of my new African family. I knew the situation by heart.

SIX WEEKS AFTER I LEFT NTHANTLHE, the village where Gen and I had our Live-In experiences, our training was officially over and our Peace Corps group moved to the Oasis Motel in Gaborone.

One morning at breakfast, I received word of Letlape's death. The family would be gathering with friends in readiness for his funeral, and I knew I needed to attend

After breakfast, I caught a bus that traveled along the Lobatse Road, skirting the border between South Africa and Botswana. I'd never ridden this bus and didn't know the area well, but I told other passengers where I was going and they helped me get off at the Otswe junction. From there, I hitchhiked the final ten miles along dusty roads.

Reaching the village, I walked the path to the Letlape's compound. Along the way, children called out, "Good morning, teacher." My white skin made me visible for a long distance and I saw guests in the yard of the compound a quarter of a mile away, turn and point in my direction.

Several Letlape sons and male relatives in blue or orange overalls sat on top of a large load of firewood behind a donkey-drawn wagon. They had parked the wagon in the shade of a morula tree and talked loudly, joked, and waved at me. Inside the *lolwapa* (yard) another group of men stoked fires where goats were roasting on spits over the coals. The fires created hardly any smoke, but filled the air with sharp incense having a fragrance like mahogany.

The family compound was not large, barely room for the three small huts. Inside the low mud wall, even a dozen people made a crowd, but on this day, sixty people massed in the lolwapa. Women crowded into the shade at one side of the house where they sat on plaid wool blankets. Young men in colorful soccer jerseys tapped a ball between them. Butsile tended to several kettles of food cooking over a fire. She stirred a huge pot of cabbage, interrupted herself to check the progress of the cornmeal *mealies* (porridge) — and salted gravy simmering in another kettle to one side of the log fire. Even so, she and I waved greetings to each other. She called to an adolescent girl to bring a bowl of water for me to wash my hands. At Butsile's direction, someone else offered me a chair in the yard, but I sat for only a minute before Butsile said to me, "*A re a mmogo*." (Come with me.)

I followed her and entered a courtyard. I remembered my first time here was eight weeks earlier. I remembered Mma Letlape comforting a baby and soothing her burned hand with aloe vera. I remembered that the child had crawled into a cooking fire.

Butsile led me into the main room of the house. The room was packed with women crowded together on the floor wherever space was available. A space was made for me and a chair appeared. One other man was in the room, undoubtedly a preacher, because he wore a dark suit and starched white shirt.

I didn't see Mma Letlape until I sat down. She was seated on a mattress on the floor, wrapped in a white sheet, her bare feet extending into the center of the room. I held her hand and she told me in a quiet voice what I already knew, Rra Letlape had died.

Within a few minutes, the preacher stood up and began a sermon. For thirty minutes, we listened to fire and brimstone, then there were hymns and prayer. When the service was over, women began gossiping about village happenings. Mma Letlape, usually boisterous among friends, remained quiet, occasionally taking a pinch of snuff.

The owner of the store in the village spoke English and translated gossip for my benefit. Her name was Mrs. Poloko Dichaba and she smiled at me from across the room.

In the middle of the floor a woman wearing a green felt beret talked about her visit to the village clinic the previous week. The doctor had informed her she had high blood pressure. It was a shock and a surprise, she said, to hear that she was not healthy. In the old days, she said, everyone dressed in animal skins, no one bathed. "We were all dirty. We all had lice. But we were healthy. Now, things have changed. We dress in modern clothing. We bathe. We even eat food from Europe. No one has lice anymore. Instead, we have high blood pressure and other medical problems. In the old days, the lice probably sucked blood and kept blood pressure low. Maybe we should go back to having lice. We'd all be healthier."

As the woman in the beret spoke, others chimed in agreement. Mrs. Dichaba, translating, was speaking only to me and she made a humorous, skeptical face occasionally that seemed to say, don't take this too seriously.

Butsile had the help of an army of adolescent girls who appeared suddenly with food for everyone in the house. They brought large bowls heaped with generous servings of mealie, goat meat, and cooked cabbage.

More than once, I'd been sternly lectured by Mma Letlape about eating whatever was served, particularly at an occasion like a funeral. Nor would she let me hedge on the quantity of food I ate. Mma told me in no uncertain terms that eating a small portion was extremely bad manners.

In this meal, Butsile had cooked everything to perfection. The goat was greasy, the cabbage cooked in the fat, the mealie sticky and heavy. After only a few bites, my mouth was coated and I gagged. Out of fear of offending Mma Letlape, I did my conscientious best, but eyebrows were raised nevertheless when I put my bowl down. Mma gave me a look of strained tolerance. The bones were immediately passed to a widow who sat near the preacher's chair. By the time a girl brought a bowl and towel for me to wash, a cat in one corner of the room was having her turn with the bones.

Sitting with Mma and the others in the house was a cleansing experience for me in some mysterious way. Many of the people here were present at the village events where I felt most awkward. On this occasion, instead of being the object of ridicule, I was accepted on an equal basis. I visited for two hours and then had to hitch a ride back to the highway. Before I left, I gave Butsile a package of photographs I'd taken in the village during my stay. Seeing them, she gave a shriek that drew all the young men to look. In the circle of people crowding around, her sister-in-law noticed some of her own children posing in the pictures and started to walk away with the entire batch. Butsile shouted at her and the two women began a row, arguing and insulting one another.

The heated voices of the two women followed me as I walked away. The sun was casting long shadows as I retraced my steps toward the road. Behind me, the hill where the village sat looked as brown and dry as ever.

I didn't know when, or even if, I'd see this village again. But on my way to the road, I realized that part of me had grown up here. I'd re-newed an acquaintance with the teenager who still resides somewhere inside. Painful memories had arisen and I'd had a chance to come to terms with the death of my father. Healing had taken place here.

One of Mma Letlape's lessons in etiquette came to me. After every meal, I was supposed to say, "*Ke klotse, Mma.*" (I feel satisfied, Madam.) When Mma taught me the phrase, she dramatized it. As I said the words, I was to push out my stomach and pat it vigorously, like a man. Striding back toward the road, on my way to hitch a ride, the phrase kept repeating in my head . . . Ke klotse, Mma.

## At the Pond

THREE WEEKS AFTER we arrived in Botswana, our Peace Corps training group moved to the village of Kanye, a few miles north of the border with South Africa. We were to stay there for about five weeks of more language training and practice teaching in a secondary school. For me, teaching again felt like a relief, though it had been more than twenty years since I'd taught at a senior high . . . and in the U.S.

We stayed in a group residence where Gen and I had a thimble-sized room. Everywhere I went, I was overwhelmed by a sense of confusion. I was trying to learn the language, but had trouble penetrating the meaning of things I saw. Venturing outside of our group residence, I moved through a world I didn't understand. Going into a store, I stumbled over the new language and finally, relied on a language of gestures. I knew it was a temporary existence and, in a strange way, also found the life of an outsider invigorating. Everything was new and that seemed to sharpen my observations.

Anything I could figure out on my own I counted as a success. A store and some of the small businesses near our residence had

31

the name *"Mmakadumo"* painted on signs and I'd concluded that Mmakadumo must be the name of the neighborhood. Despite my lack of familiarity with the language and the area, I'd figured that out on my own and felt a bit smug.

At the end of each school day I walked to a nearby reservoir. The trail I followed from the residence to the reservoir led along the base of a rocky hill, through a stand of eucalyptus and into knee-high grass where cattle often grazed. The grass was dry as straw from lack of rain. Occasionally, a troop of baboons rested on the large red-streaked rocks of the hillside. As soon as they saw me, male sentinels barked a warning, females and young jumped from rock to rock in their retreat up the slope as if fleeing from a dangerous predator.

The reservoir was a watering place, possibly a hundred feet across. Because of the drought, the water level was unusually low that year and around the pond the steep bank was marked by concentric rings that showed the ebb of water during a year without rain.

A demonstration garden with a wealth of tropical fruit trees — banana, papaya, mango — grew on the south side of the pond.

A family of vervet monkeys, their serious faces fringed with white, hid in the taller trees. They chattered, waiting for a chance to steal bananas. But as soon as I appeared, the monkeys began to scream and scold from above. They seemed to single me out, as if spotting my white skin they were convinced I'd come to torment them in some way.

The place was alive with village children and livestock. Young boys, still in their elementary school uniforms — khaki shorts and short sleeved shirts — brought their family's goats or cattle to the pond, then played games while the animals went for the water. At first the animals dashed to get to the pond, but the steep, muddy slope made the approach treacherous. Near the edge, their legs sank into the soft earth. Most approached the water at a spot that was not so steep and where a path had been trampled. Though thirsty, they all paused before heading down the bank to study the slope and take account of the ways the mud could betray them.

Further on, almost opposite the fruit trees, bones of a cow were imbedded in the muck. Apparently desperate for water during the long dry spell, the beast had gone down the steeper slope and become stuck. Its rib cage and spine were clearly visible, the skull was set at a grotesque angle. Scavengers had picked the bones clean, and now they served as a caution for the other animals that there was danger here.

AFTER VISITING THE POND almost daily for several weeks, one day I met a tall, copper-skinned youth. The fourteen-year-old was dressed in his secondary school uniform, a short sleeved white shirt and navy blue slacks. We were both sauntering around the reservoir and when we passed within a few feet of each other, I recognized him. He made no sign of noticing me and would not have spoken, except for my greeting. "Dumela," I said. "You are a student at the secondary school where I am teaching." I carefully chose my words in English, speaking them as clearly as possible. "Do you live close by?"

The fellow looked at me, paused, and said, "A short distance away." He waved his right hand in a vague direction.

The young man's English was excellent, but his reserved demeanor surprised me. Perhaps, I expected him to register delight at the attention, instead, his response seemed aloof.

"Does the pond have a name?" I asked the question mainly, to make conversation. I didn't really think it had a name.

However, the young man paused as if my question deserved a lengthy deliberation. After a long silence, he said, "This place is called Mmakadumo Dam."

The name made sense to me because it seemed to refer to the area I thought of as the Mmakadumo district. Making this connection and recognizing the name, I suddenly felt a glow of pride.

The young man maintained a long silence, still studying me and apparently considering whether it was all right to speak to me, before he began to explain. "When I was young, I was not supposed to come here. My aunt and uncle told me a story when I was little," he said. "Mmakadumo is a giant snake. He captures children near the edge of the reservoir. Then, drags them into the water and they disappear forever."

It was interesting, I thought, that businesses near my residence had taken the name of a snake. The Africans I knew hated snakes.

The young man relaxed enough to walk with me and began to tell me about his life. As we circled the pond, he told me his name was Molifi. He had no brothers or sisters and never knew his father. Molifi lived alone for weeks at a time because his mother worked in a clothing shop in the next village. Most of his food came from lunches provided to students at school.

He mentioned that he was almost finished with school and, even if he passed tests for entry to a senior secondary school, his mother would not be able to afford the fees. More than likely, he told me, this would be the last year of his education. Molifi described the details of his life with an attitude of acceptance, that this is the way life is. The more I listened to his gentle voice, the more astounded I became by the level of understanding and depth in his words. I was struck by the contrast between our lives. Molifi didn't have basic things I'd always taken for granted: family support, regular meals, or even a future that included education.

We continued our slow pace around the pond. We passed by the demonstration garden with its bounty of fruit. Further on I gazed at the white bones of the unlucky cow imbedded in the mud. I must have stared at it too long, transfixed by the sight of the skeleton.

"I saw that beast die," Molifi said in a detached way. "It died slowly. For two or three days it struggled in the mud."

"The cow belonged to someone, didn't it?" I asked. "Didn't the owner help?"

"The farmer came once," he said, "but in the end, the animal was abandoned."

We talked about school and Molifi confided that he had a crush on one of the Peace Corps teachers. She was an American woman who spoke kindly to him and gave him food. On Saturdays he could go to her lodging for a meal. Once, when he was sick, she took him to the clinic. His voice became more animated as he talked about her. "I hope she will take me to America when she goes home," he said.

We walked in silence for a minute before I heard Molifi clear his throat.

He said, "There is something more about Mmakadumo Dam I didn't tell you. My aunt warned me that I should stay away because Mmakadumo might come out of the water in disguise. Instead of looking like a snake, sometimes he changed his shape to look like a white man. He gained the trust of young children with gentle words. Then he kidnapped them, took them to the bottom of the reservoir, and ate them. Families never saw their children again, but they always knew Mmakadumo had taken them."

Molifi looked at me with a sly grin. "Maybe it's not polite to tell that to a white man. I'm too old to believe those stories." We were walking through straw-colored grass and he suddenly seemed embarrassed. His expression turned into a smile of apology. "When I first met you," he said, "I didn't want to speak. I thought you might be Mmakadumo."

I didn't quite know how to react to the revelation about a monster in the guise of a white man. Especially the detail that I might have been the monster. Molifi was too old to believe the story, but I could see that he believed it anyway.

At first, it jolted me to hear him relate his aunt's warning. I was full of the ideals of being a Peace Corps Volunteer and the values of education, none of which, of course, had anything to do with kidnapping children. Momentarily, I felt defensive. Hearing the warning against trusting a white man, I felt implicated. But, I reminded myself, we were very close to South Africa where the repressive rules of Apartheid had echoes. Also, I knew that many families have connections on both sides of the border. Visiting in South Africa, people would feel the sting of Apartheid. Remembering those things, the story began to seem protective. The aunt and uncle told Molifi the story to teach him about the world as they had experienced it.

As Molifi and I had been talking, shadows had grown longer. I began to notice that the air was cooling off, as it does in the desert.

It was time for me to head back to the teachers' residence and Molifi wanted to walk with me. He was smiling broadly on his way to see the American teacher who had been so nice to him. I knew the woman. She was tall, blond, and had a kind disposition. I could see that in doing favors for Molifi, she'd raised his expectations. I also knew, that like me, she'd be leaving in about two weeks to work in a village somewhere else in Botswana. I hoped everything would turn out alright for her and for Molifi.

Molifi's story about Mmakadumo weighed on my mind. I'd learned the true meaning of the name Mmakadumo: that it is dangerous to speak to a white man. I hadn't realized the depth of distrust here.

As I thought about his story, I began to see Molifi in a new light. Understanding the reason for his aloofness earlier, I realized he'd had to summon his courage and had taken quite a risk in order to talk to me.

Before we left the reservoir, I turned back for one last glance and to get my bearings in the strange surroundings. Sunlight glistened across the water and on the far slope the whitened skull seemed to scowl like a mask. Two goats stood at the edge of the pond, pausing before stepping into the hazardous mud.

I'd come to teach. Everything in Africa was new to me, but already I saw that the footing could be perilous here.

**JANUARY 1991**

to

**JUNE 1991**

## Unhinged (Temporarily)

### I

IT WAS ON A THURSDAY that we traveled about 435 kilometers from Gaborone in the south of the country, north to Francistown in a bus with a large group of teachers assigned to work in the region.

The next day, Gen and I, along with fifteen other teachers who would also be working in Tonota, the village where we would live for the next two years, rode the final 32 kilometers there in the back of an open livestock truck. In the truck most of us stood shoulder-to-shoulder, baggage at our feet. A few people sat on suitcases. My impression was that all of us were trying to make sense of what was happening — I know I was!

The truck stopped at every school in Tonota and gradually most of the teachers — Africans from several different countries, a couple from India, a man from Bangladesh, two Brits, and another Peace Corps Volunteer — had been dropped off.

Each time the truck arrived at a school, I observed a similar scene. The headmaster — or his deputy — meets the truck as the new teacher climbs down. His good manners require him to stifle his surprise when he hears the teacher describe his or her qualifications: "You teach math? Well, I asked the Ministry for an English teacher. I already have five people who teach math. But, welcome. Let's see what we can work out."

I heard variations on this conversation repeated a dozen times, until just three of us were left in the truck bed — Gen, a man from Uganda, and myself.

The Ugandan was a young man, tall and good looking, with very black skin. We had traveled through the village together for several hours by that time, and more than once I'd tried to initiate a conversation with him, but he was alone and barely able to contain his fear. He recoiled from my overtures, conveying a sense that it was no time for small talk.

At that point there was plenty of room to sit, but it was uncomfortable. With rattling and bouncing on the rough road, I preferred to stand and inhale the smell of dust and dung and wood smoke, the distant smell of rain, and occasionally, a whiff of desert sage.

A single cloud hung low and dark over the far half of Tonota, but the sun, peeking around the perimeter, baked down on us. The further away from the highway the truck carried us, the more I could see of the village spread over a long, gradual hillside. There must have been a thousand of the round mud huts with thatch roofs — *rondevaals*, as they are called — laid out on the sloping, sandy landscape. A few thorn trees were visible, acacias with their distinct flat-topped profile. As we traveled deeper into the heart of the village, a rock-filled riverbed ran parallel to the road — completely dry, and it looked as if it had been for some time.

Close to the road, women collected water at a tap and carried it on their heads in yellow anti-freeze cans or plastic jugs. Children played near the round huts, but no toys were visible. They played with homemade clay animals or they jumped rope, but most of the children sat still along the side of the road watching the truck roll past. At the sight of white faces, some cried out, "Good morning, teacher!"

Above the rondevaals, a dozen eagles circled. With no visible movement of their huge wings, they traced a continuous path over the village, like a form of perpetual motion.

Cattle, untended as far as I could detect, marched in a purposeful line along the road. Flocks of goats wandered, scrambling here and there, accompanied by young boys with long sticks. Seeing the old houses and the traditional way of life I felt a curious satisfaction. It all seemed to represent something authentic and very old.

As the truck rolled through the village, even the sand on the road looked ancient. There surely was automobile traffic here, but all I could see were hoof prints in the sand from the thousands of animals that used this road. The prints of livestock obliterated every trace of vehicles. I know they don't last long, but seeing the prints left by hooves, I had a sense of the cycles of village life. The daily march of animals to their watering place, and later, their return to the kraal. Hoof prints blown by the wind. Sand and fresh dung trampled under hooves. Wind shifting fine particles until the prints are erased. Only the sand remains to tell the story.

SINCE I'D COME TO AFRICA to make changes in my life, I was keenly aware of the irony of traveling to another continent in order to report to a junior secondary school to which I was recently assigned. It was *exactly* the way I started teaching thirty years earlier. Later on, I was scheduled to move to the teachers' college, but that would have to wait until the second-year students returned from practice teaching.

Even so, the secondary school felt like a huge obstacle and I kept asking myself, *do I have to do that all over again? Is this the kind of change I want?*

Thirty years earlier, in Seattle, I stepped into a middle school classroom. I had worked hard for the opportunity to be a teacher.

For several years as a student in the College of Education, I'd cobbled together a series of fly-by-night jobs to pay for room, board, and tuition, working in restaurants and gas stations, in a mill where I mixed dog food, and on a corporate yacht where I polished the brass and did the cooking. For a few months, I greased machinery and swept the floor where they made chocolate-covered mints sold door to door by Campfire Girls. I did singing commercials for an FM radio station and worked as a clown at shopping mall openings. Before I became a teacher, I'd even done a stint in the local juvenile detention center — the "groovy joovy," we called it — as a supervisor and recreation teacher.

I had the beginnings of a family by the time I started my job as a teacher — my son was a year old — and even though I didn't make quite enough money to pay the bills, I thought of teaching as my career. It was what I was going to do with my life. But midway through my first semester at the school, my necktie choked me and the headmaster scolded me. He called me into his office one day to tell me the shirt I was wearing was "non-professional attire." He was criticizing my best shirt — ivory in color, Oxford fabric, with a button down collar. He informed me that the school had a policy for male teachers, white shirts only.

That first term, I stood outside my room in-between classes supervising the hallway, as all the teachers were required to do, and got to know the fellow who taught in the room next door. He was the basketball coach, a veteran math teacher, and twenty years older than me. His puffy eyes always seemed half-closed. He seldom made direct eye contact, and I began to realize that he was either totally burned out, hung-over, or both. At the time, I began to ask myself, do I want to feel that way twenty years from now?

That was when I came to realize the job I'd worked so hard to qualify for was, very likely, not a job that I could enjoy forever, but it was a long-term, temporary career.

AS GEN AND I BOUNCED through Tonota for the first time, housing was definitely on our minds. We needed to restore a sense of stability to our lives and having a house would be a positive step. It had been eight months since we'd moved out of our house in Seattle and we had been living out of a suitcase for far too long. During our training period, we had been in various living situations, mostly some variation on a dorm room.

From time to time we shared a romantic daydream of living in a rondevaal. After all, they were everywhere in the village. In our dreaming, we overlooked a few details, of course. Rondevaals lacked electricity and running water, but at least we'd be in a house. I was tired of being in one brief arrangement after another. Neither of us knew exactly where we'd find a place to live. We did know that housing was scarce and was provided by the schools.

Of course, we'd left all of our household belongings behind in America, and as we entered the village in the truck, Gen was sitting on a red duffel bag that contained everything we owned in Botswana. But when I looked at what the man from Uganda carried, I realized we had brought much more than we needed. In one hand he held a thin briefcase, under his arm — a blanket, and his other hand clutched the rolled end of a clear plastic bag containing a dinner plate and utensils — a knife, a fork, and a spoon. Until that moment, I thought we'd done well in paring down our belongings to the bare necessities.

THE PAVEMENT ENDED and after a few kilometers of rough deep sand, we passed a boundary . . . there were no more houses and the village merged into scrub trees and *bushveld* (sub-tropical woodland). Two kilometers further the truck made a turn that led into a paved parking lot. We passed under an archway with a sign that read, Tonota College of Education. Construction trucks were parked in one corner and bricklayers worked to complete a wall on the edge of the campus.

"This must be where you're headed," I said to the Ugandan.

He said nothing, but raised his eyebrows and flickered a silent assent with his eyes. We stopped in front of the administrative office and the representative from the Ministry who had been accompanying us stepped out of the cab and entered the building.

As we waited, the Ugandan climbed down over the tailgate. He stood on the pavement when the Ministry official returned accompanied by an older man, a tall, paunchy African wearing shirt sleeves, whom he introduced as the deputy principal of the college — this position is comparable to the vice president in a U.S. college.

Apparently, our arrival had interrupted him at work in his office. His round prominent eyes glared at the Ugandan, then at Gen and me still in the truck. He seemed irritated at having to waste his precious time on any of us.

I watched the man with interest. I'd worked in enough schools and colleges to know that the man designated as number two, the deputy in his case, was the person assigned unpleasant chores. I knew many people in his position who were capable of being aggressive or even nasty, and who displayed a thin-skinned insensitivity as a form of professional certification.

The Ugandan seemed very alone and vulnerable at that moment. His face remained completely impassive as he gave his shoulders a little shake in preparation to introduce himself. The deputy, however, wasted no time on pleasantries. Instead of introducing himself, he asked, "Are you sure you belong here? To my knowledge, we have received no correspondence from the Ministry." His manner seemed unnecessarily challenging and abrupt.

The Ugandan's gaze met the eyes of the deputy and he replied, "My letter of introduction and curriculum vitae were to have been sent by the Ministry." His accent was African with the unmistakable overtones of British English. In a former British territory like Botswana, the superior tone of a British accent is often the best defense against surly bureaucrats. The young man showed no sign of backing down.

"I find myself at a disadvantage," the deputy said, feigning vulnerability. "The principal is away and I have had no prior warning that we were to expect a new teacher. What do you teach?" His brows wrinkled in disbelief that a man this young could teach anything at all.

The young man was obviously tired. It was afternoon already and our group of teachers had been travelling since early morning. His shoulders slumped visibly, but his face betrayed no fear.

"Education. Mediated instruction, sir."

"And you have a master's degree?" The deputy made no effort to hide his sarcasm.

"Yes, sir." He shifted his left arm slightly where the rolled blanket was still tucked.

"Where did you graduate?" asked the deputy, standing with hands on his hips, wearing a fierce expression.

"Oxford, sir."

"When?"

"I passed exams in June."

"Well," the deputy said, still dubious, "I suppose the thing to do is give you housing, at least for the weekend. We may return you to Gaborone for the Ministry to straighten out your situation. I'll call the driver Monday to take you, if need be."

The deputy seemed to have no more feeling about returning the man to Gaborone than he would about returning a letter delivered by mistake. But finally, he turned and, with the Ugandan, walked towards the office building to make arrangements.

The truck started up and we drove on.

IT WAS A SHORT DISTANCE to the community junior secondary school where I'd been temporarily assigned. At the entrance to the school grounds, a gate swung open on hinges between two large concrete block posts, and a sign announced Lethlabile CJSS. Beyond the gate, the truck bounced along on a dusty driveway between the school and a semicircle of teachers' houses, all cream-yellow, concrete-block structures.

The driver stopped the truck in front of the school, and the Ministry of Education official, who had been accompanying us, got out of the truck cab and disappeared into the administrative office. I waited near the truck studying a chain-link goat fence that encircled the school grounds.

Within a few minutes I was invited inside for an interview with the headmaster, Mr. M'nkundla, a tall, middle-aged Zimbabwean with the complexion of light coffee. He spoke excellent English with a rich African accent and, of course, in our interview he wanted to know something about my past. I told him about my teaching experience and as I talked, his eyes met mine with a direct steady gaze. He listened, and I discovered that I liked the man. By the time we had finished our short conversation, I knew I could make the best of the assignment to this school, even if it was a short-term position.

OUR LAST STOP in Tonota was to be at Gen's school, where, we had been informed during training, there would be housing available for us.

When we arrived, the headmaster informed Gen that there were already three home-ec teachers on the staff, and he and Gen would have to meet with the other teachers to see what classes were available.

Then he told us, "You'll have to share a house with another teacher." To help us feel better about it, he added, "It's only a temporary arrangement."

The headmaster was a tall, rotund man with an outgoing, jolly manner that made me think of a used car salesman. "I'll get right to work and find a house for you," he told us.

In retrospect, I think he meant "there are no houses in the area and I have no idea what to do with you." But we had no way of knowing that at the time.

IT WAS MID-AFTERNOON, and the air was muggy and hot when we arrived at our temporary new house. Our housemate was Berna Modiko, a light-skinned *Motswana* (Botswanan) woman; she wore a conservative Western-style brown dress that buttoned up the front. Welcoming us, she smiled, brushed her dress with her hands, and fussed a little with her Afro. I realized later what a brave gesture it was on Berna's part to welcome us into her home. Our invasion of her little house must have left her quite distraught, but that afternoon she was very gracious.

Berna was an open-minded young woman and had agreed to the headmaster's request to share her house, in part because a year or two earlier, she'd lived with another Peace Corps Volunteer, a young, single woman, and they'd become good friends. We all knew immediately that sharing a house with a middle-aged couple might be another matter entirely for her.

Berna was thoughtful. She took time in conversations to listen, and make considered responses. Berna also seemed to have been exposed to Western culture — more so than many Africans whom I had met.

Her English was excellent, she spoke Setswana with her friends, and when the three of us went to a small grocery in the village, Berna immediately switched to speaking fluent Afrikaans with the owners, who were mixed-race women from South Africa.

Our shared house was typical of those made available to teachers. It had a small, sandy yard, and was provided with electricity and a gas stove. There was solar-powered hot water, and Berna owned a small fridge.

The place seemed adequate in every way, though it wasn't until we unpacked that we realized how small our quarters were. The bedroom where we were to stay was just big enough for a small bed. With two people and luggage, we felt like sardines in a tin. Our circumstances in the small room were certainly not Berna's fault. None of us had much choice in the matter, and we all tried to make the best of the situation.

The house, surrounded by trees and greenery, was in a convenient location as we were a stone's throw from the highway to Francistown.

On the Saturday night of our first weekend, Berna had invited friends to the house — another woman and three young men — to have a party before school started. In the hours Gen and I were trying to sleep, they prepared food, had a late night dinner, played music on the radio, and danced into the wee hours. Our schedules were not a good match.

Though Gen and I are not church goers, Sunday morning we joined Berna and her friends in going to a church in Francistown. It was a bilingual service in a Pentecostal Christian church, and two ministers danced around the podium as they took turns delivering simultaneous sermons, one in Setswana, the other in English. I especially enjoyed the gospel music.

We got to know Berna during that first weekend. She welcomed us to participate in the late night gathering, but we were simply at different points in our lives. In middle age, Gen and I were no longer interested in all-night parties with lots of music, food, and friends. We'd become morning people, which meant early evenings for us.

**II**

MONDAY MORNING MY ALARM woke me up at four-thirty a.m. I'd set it early in order to have enough time to get across the village to my school. Five and a half miles — which I translated as eight or nine kilometers — lay between me and my school.

From the narrow bed I could see the duffel bag in the corner of the small room where my clean clothes would be. Nearby, Gen was still asleep. The previous night, Berna and her friends had played music on a boom box turned up full volume. It was the first day of the term and I hadn't slept much, but groggy or not, I needed an early start.

In the dim light as I stepped out of the bedroom, I could see bodies of the partiers everywhere, people sleeping on the floor. Heading in to pour my bath, I had to step gingerly.

I left the house wearing a navy blue blazer, maroon necktie, blue shirt, and cotton suntans — the prescribed wardrobe for a teacher in Botswana. The air was still and dark, light growing steadily in the east. A few puffy clouds glowed in the sky. Within fifteen minutes I reached the main road, and, in the growing predawn light, a *combi* appeared. I heard the whine of the ancient Volkswagen engine long before I saw it. Combis in Botswana, were VW vans with seats arranged to provide space for twenty passengers. I waved to flag him down and the driver started to pull over, but inexplicably he changed his mind and didn't stop.

I traveled on foot through the village that morning and watched the sky turn a brilliant orange. The sun hadn't yet appeared, but the light seemed enough to warm the air. I could imagine the sun, rising over the highlands of Zimbabwe to the east. The mental picture of the sun in Zimbabwe seemed to make the morning more of an exotic adventure.

As the light grew, roosters of the village began to crow, then dogs began to bark. Donkeys brayed. Cows and goats joined in, as well, until the noise reached a crescendo and the first rays of sunlight streamed across the roofs of rondevaals. The flame finally appeared in the east signaling to the animals that their duty had been accomplished and the chorus subsided.

After the raucous dawn chorus, the entire village now seemed blanketed in a deeper silence. A few doves cooed in the trees, but everything was quiet by the time I reached my destination eighty minutes from the time I'd begun.

The school day began at 6:40 a.m. with four hundred students lining up on the grounds in ragged rows near a flagpole for the morning assembly; the warmth of the air increased by the minute as everybody gathered in the slanting rays of the early morning sun.

My walk to school had already warmed me up — I was perspiring heavily. All the students wore school uniforms — light blue dresses for the girls, the boys in sky blue shirts and navy trousers. Many had rolled out of bed and run to school, boys' shirt tails hung loosely, white t-shirts were untucked, belts loose, dresses not fully buttoned. I stood near the office building in the midst of a group of teachers and we looked on as the headmaster, immaculate in a sport coat, slacks and tie, waited for students to line up by class, before he walked to the center of the grounds.

It had been a few days since I'd met Mr. M'nkundla for our brief interview and I hardly knew him. But I found myself wondering about the carefully groomed man standing now before the somewhat, raggle-taggle student body.

I couldn't help comparing the assembly to my early days in a middle school near Seattle. That first day in a Botswana school the students displayed a range of skin color from deep brown to nearly white, with shades of mahogany, copper, and caramel brown thrown into the mix. The school population I'd seen thirty years earlier, with the exception of one Asian teacher, was all white-skinned.

I was much younger then and unsure of myself. I puzzled constantly over how to behave in my new role as a teacher. In my search for models, of course, invariably I looked in the wrong places. The principal, head of the family of teachers and students who populated the middle school where I worked, dispensed norms of behavior from a textbook he'd run across in an education class years earlier. As a model for behavior, he was a total disaster. The man was a martinet — rigid in his response to any crisis, unbending in his devotion to rules, and inflexible until the superintendent issued an order. The principal lasted five months before the teaching staff mutinied and he was moved to a desk somewhere in an office downtown.

That morning in Botswana, I was interested to see the course Mr. M'nkundla would take with the four hundred students and twenty teachers standing on the school grounds.

His eyes made a sweep of the gathered student body and, suddenly, a frown — a very subtle movement of his eyebrows — came over his face. He didn't say a word, but the lines of students began to straighten out under the power of his gaze. Within the space of a breath, tails were hastily tucked, buttons buttoned, belts buckled, posture straightened.

For a minute, everyone stood in silence, then, from somewhere in the throng of students, a high-pitched voice sang out a first line to begin a hymn. In my experience, public schools didn't profess religion, but the singing that morning was both mysterious and beautiful. The students sang an English hymn set to an African melody, an example of the pervasive influence of the London Missionary Society in southern Africa. The students sang in four-part harmony, yet no one needed to teach or lead. Everyone knew their part and where they belonged — a basic rule of life in an African village put into practice.

The singing ended and Mr. M'nkundla began, "The Lord is my shepherd . . .," leading students in a recitation. How many of these students herd livestock after school? I wondered. Clearly, pastoral images spoke directly to them.

Then he read from the Psalms:

> The works of the Lord are great . . .
> He hath given meat unto them that fear him
> He will be ever mindful of his covenant.
> The works of his hands are truth and judgment;
> all his commandments are sure.

"What this passage means," he said, "is that fear of the Lord is the beginning of wisdom. God provides food to those who fear him and gives food to those who are seeking wisdom."

As the headmaster spoke, a noisy stirring passed through the assembly. It was obvious that biblical passages didn't play some vague purpose, like spiritual guidance. Everything had a concrete meaning. Any mention of food was a reminder to students why they were here.

For many, the only meal of the day would be the lunch provided at the secondary school.

He continued to hammer on the theme. "Meat or food," he said, "can be understood as the goal of the wisdom we seek in school." He had their complete attention. "Meat or food" was the reason for being in school. Many of these adolescents, the ones who succeeded in finishing their education, would be guaranteed a steady supply of meat and food by being able to secure employment.

"In getting an education you are getting the greatest food the Lord provides — food for thought. Wisdom." He looked up and surveyed the lines of students, giving them a moment to reflect on his theme: the promise of food.

"Because your teachers are here to help you get an education . . . help you attain wisdom . . . they are acting on the Lord's behalf. I want you to think today about obedience to your teachers. I want you to respect your teachers and to have reverence for the wisdom they impart."

In other words, the school acted on behalf of God, providing meat and food. Headmaster and teachers are agents of the deity.

My feet shuffled involuntarily in the sand as I listened. It disturbed me to hear religious teachings expressed this way. Though I found it unsettling, I realized at the same time it was a message well within the boundaries of the culture.

I reminded myself that this kind of pitch — a motivational talk setting behavioral norms — is always cultural. In many secondary schools in America, achievement in athletics, not the Bible, sets the standard. One time I heard a principal in Seattle delivering a morning talk that he ended with an aphorism: "Remember," he said, "the difference between a champ and a chump is the letter U."

I made a conscious effort to keep my mind open. The headmaster had a complex task, conveying behavioral expectations, citing a text from ancient Judaic culture to an audience of adolescents in southern Africa. And, he was making a double-edged point, motivating students as well as reminding the teachers — young, and mostly inexperienced — of the higher goals of their occupation.

LATER THAT MORNING during our tea break in the staffroom, I had my first chance to introduce myself to some of the young teachers.

I met Duncan, a science teacher from Zambia, and my first impression was of the depth of his sensitivity and intelligence. Duncan was from an area known as the Copper Belt that lay along the border of the Congo, and like most of the residents of Central Africa, his skin was a deep brown, almost black. He told me he'd been in the army once, during a time when there'd been a coup in Angola and several armies confronted each other. The Zambian army was brought into the conflict, and Duncan saw combat against a Cuban force, various rebel groups, and the South African Defense Force. Duncan had an almost pedantic style of speaking English as he told me, "How surprised I was to look through the sights of my rifle and see another man, just as frightened as I. In the Zambian army, we never knew who we were firing at. I had a very sick feeling all the time I was there. I wanted to go home as fast as I could."

Duncan had been married less than a year. He and his wife had a baby girl, two months old. "My wife and I came from different villages," he told me. "Our families brought us together and we met only a few days before we were married. Our only problem is, we speak different languages. In the part of Zambia we are from, every village has a different tribe and every tribe its own language. My wife didn't speak much English when we met. And besides, English is for business or education. It's not used in homes. So, for a year, I've been trying to learn to speak her language." Duncan had a small notebook tucked among a stack of books near him. He pulled it out to show me. "In my study of her language, I take notes here. When I go home, she's *my* teacher." He chuckled.

Later in the day, there was a break for lunch, a two-hour pause. Afterward, students would return to classrooms for a study period

until four, and then sports activities would keep us all in school until approximately 6:00 p.m. There wasn't time for me to return to
Berna's house during the break, so I decided to rest in the staffroom.

Duncan came through the door and saw me trying to doze sitting
up in a chair. "You have no place to go," he said. "Come to my house."
His invitation wasn't a question. He wore a sympathetic expression
on his face and I liked the man. How could I refuse?

He and his wife were housed in one of the small concrete-block
houses within the school grounds. Duncan led me through the front
door saying, "Come in. We have food prepared in the kitchen."

As soon as he said that, I began to wonder, how could this happen? But I followed him into the kitchen where a small table was set
with two plates of steaming food. "My wife is in the bedroom with
the child." He motioned toward a closed door. Then he said, "Sit
down. Make yourself at home."

I was overwhelmed by his hospitality and puzzled, as well. For a
minute, Duncan disappeared into the bedroom to see his wife and his
daughter. I heard his voice through the door and I liked the sound of
the language he was speaking, though I couldn't understand a word.
Nor did I hear any response from his wife.

Duncan returned, smiling, and took a seat across the orange
Formica tabletop. The food on the plate was a maize-meal porridge
called *bogobe*, or *paleche* in Botswana, but a hundred different words
are used for the same traditional African meal in other countries. It
was topped with a gravy of cabbage and goat meat. Often the meal
is eaten with the fingers of the right hand instead of utensils, but out
of consideration, Duncan gave me a soup spoon. I thanked him for
his hospitality, and we began our meal.

I had had a momentary thought . . . when I first entered the
kitchen, that Duncan was being led astray by his own goodwill. My
first impression was that these two plates of food were set out for
Duncan and his wife. But he was so gracious and it was too late for
me to refuse. His wife remained in the bedroom. I neither saw her

nor heard any word from her while I was at their house. That day was the first time he invited me to his house for a noon meal . . . and it was, also, the last. My guess is that Duncan's wife later gave him a language lesson he couldn't forget.

IT WAS HOT THAT FIRST DAY at the school and as I walked between desks in my classroom assisting students, perspiration dripped from my coat sleeve down my wrists. By mid-morning I'd hung up my jacket. Before the week ended, I quit wearing the jacket altogether. Friday, I walked into the staffroom and overheard teachers discussing my breach of protocol. "He can't take the heat," one said. Another answered, "You must understand, he's from a cold climate."

Eventually, the trust that students placed in me buoyed my spirits. They looked to me as someone who was going to help them learn English and pass exams. Also, I found that I enjoyed the give and take in the secondary school classroom and the flexibility required to keep the class moving.

But during that first week of classes, I had a serious problem. On Monday, I had the students go to a blackboard and write out vocabulary words. I wanted to learn their names and associate names with faces. But when I called out student's names, many of them didn't respond.

The problem was, they didn't know what I was saying when I tried to pronounce their names. One girl, for example, was named Ruth. I had identified Ruth as exactly the kind of student middle school teachers appreciate having in class — she was cooperative, helpful, and bright. But, when I called on her, she sat in her seat, oblivious.

The obstacle in this apparently simple communication was my American "r." In Africa, it was a strange sound and students didn't know what to make of it. I realized I had to work on my ability to pronounce my "r's." The sound has to be rolled energetically, a thick trill of the tongue off the front teeth. Walking home from school, I practiced the sound making a noise as if I was playing a child's game

55

with a model airplane. Every day that week, I practiced until I got it right. Still, my American accent continued to amaze and amuse my students.

After that first week, students knew when I was calling on them to do something in class. But long after they had gotten used to my accent, on occasion I saw students glance at one another and snicker when they heard me pronounce the "r" sound.

ON SATURDAY, a week after we arrived in Tonota, Gen and I went into Francistown to buy a bicycle. The bike we found was a Grailey Rabbit Racer made in China. The center bar had a decal that pictured a Chinese version of a Bugs Bunny type of character. The bike was black, one speed, with balloon tires. I rode it to school on Monday and, right away, experienced the luxury of coasting part of the way.

On my daily commute across the village, I traveled the same road we'd driven our first day. Early on, I'd guessed it was an ancient route.

■

Later I read in the Francistown library that the road did, indeed, have a long history. In some books it was referred to as Missionary Road. It had been used by the missionaries of southern Africa to travel north as they made contact with new tribal groups.

As a medical missionary David Livingstone used this road on his exploratory trips in the 1840s, but the road had existed long before missionaries arrived.

In the nineteenth century, the Boers of South Africa and the *Tswana* [indigenous people of Botswana and elsewhere in Southern Africa] fought bitterly over a boundary between South Africa and the territory then known as Bechuanaland — now, Botswana. Boer commandos regularly made slave raids into the area. Livingstone, and other missionaries connected to the London Missionary Society, actively opposed slavery and the Boers suspected that missionaries were delivering arms to various tribal groups. They wanted this road to be a boundary so they'd have more control over its use.

In the 1880s and 1890s, Cecil Rhodes — diamond magnate, politician, real estate promoter, and eventual founder of the Rhodes Scholarship — built the original railroad in the area following the route of Missionary Road, in order to bring white farmers into his vast domain — Rhodesia — modern day Zimbabwe.

■

It was a relief to have my balloon-tired bicycle to travel Missionary Road, but not a pure blessing. For one thing, I had to deal with frequent flat tires. Thorn seeds, that lay hidden in the sand, were hard, with several spiked points, any one of which could do in a bike tire. I went to great lengths to protect the tires, eventually doubling the inner tubes.

In the morning, when I arrived at school, I leaned my bike against a wall near the door of the teachers' staff room, but very quickly, I realized it was too accessible. One of the teachers used it at various times in the day if he had an errand. Of course, he didn't ask my permission, and having anyone use my bike was a concern.

The first time the fellow borrowed it, my face must have registered surprise or displeasure. But that didn't faze him in the least. "We share with our brothers," he said. "It's the African way."

The next day, he used the bike and later I found him applying a patch to the front tire. "I ran over a thorn," he explained. "But Africans return things in the same condition they find them."

Later in the week, the same thing happened, but my favorable opinion of him gained several points when, true to his word, he again repaired the tire. A week later, I saw him ride off as I was walking to class. It's okay, I told myself. I'll be in class and the bike will be returned by the time I need it. At the end of the school day, I found it leaning against the wall. The back tire was flat and the fellow avoided me for several days.

WE'D BEEN IN BERNA'S HOUSE for almost two weeks, and due to the limited space, the level of friction was rising and becoming more of an issue. The constant stream of conflicting activity — cooking and entertaining versus sleeping — meant it was hard for the three of us to not feel frustrated and slightly irritated at each other.

The headmaster at Gen's school had told us when we first arrived, he would locate housing, and during the second week he told us, "I found a vacant house. " He hadn't seen it yet, he said, but the owner had given him permission to show it to us.

The next afternoon, we rode in the headmaster's truck to see the place, but stepping through the front door was like entering a bad dream. Inside the unpainted gray stone house, empty metal window frames were stacked in the living room; none of the windows had been installed. On one side of the main room, we saw the promise of a kitchen: a rudimentary counter, without plumbing and no stove. It was hard to tell if something might be about to happen, or whether someone had walked off the job. Outside, the owner had dug a deep pit at one end of the house, perhaps attempting to install an indoor toilet. The hole was twelve feet square and filled with poisonous looking green water, thick with mosquito larvae.

The experience forced us to make a decision. We had reached our limit in the current living situation, and things were on edge. It was clearly time to take matters into our own hands. Since I was scheduled to teach at Tonota College of Education in a few months, I went to the college to inquire about housing, and immediately I was offered a house on the campus. We moved in the next weekend.

After the move, it became Gen's turn to do a daily commute across the village. Within a few weeks, however, she was able to resolve that problem by working out a transfer and very soon she began teaching at the same school where I worked. The energy-draining commute was over for both of us.

# III

IT WAS A BIG STEP when Gen and I finally moved into a house of our own. After moving there, I wanted to feel a measure of stability, but it took time before I was able to relax. The previous few months had been intense. Nothing was certain and there was nothing to hold onto. It took some time for me to work through the accumulated tension and get to a less stressful state. Through it all, I often puzzled, *I'm getting the fresh start I'd wanted, but why is it that it is all so confusing?*

Both of us had busy schedules that included after-school meetings, too many student workbooks to mark, and extracurricular duties at school. I'd been assigned the job of coordinating English teachers at the secondary school and Gen was busy organizing her home economics lab for exams. I was at school for nearly twelve hours every day and my work took a toll.

I was stressed out.

The week after Gen and I moved into our new house, I took a walk on the road with another teacher named Tim during our lunch break. Tim was an Aussie, and the one other Westerner on the staff at the school.

As we walked I saw something in the dust a few feet ahead of us. "Look. What's this? A dead snake," I said. "What kind is it?" I asked. "Do you know?"

Tim and I bent to get a closer look. The body was about a foot-and-a-half long with pinkish skin. Dark dots of pigmentation on the back made a diamond pattern. Against the red sand, the colors blended perfectly.

"It's an immature cobra," he told me. "An Egyptian cobra."

After Tim turned the snake over with his foot, he said, "We had a bunch of them at the school last year. A nest hatched somewhere on the school grounds. The snakes were tiny, but lethal, and they all tried to take cover in student lockers. The deputy headmaster had the faculty and staff cleaning cobras out of lockers for an entire afternoon, but none of the *Batswana* [people of Botswana] teachers would help and the students were pretty much petrified."

"Teachers wouldn't help?"

Tim shook his head. "Snakes aren't exactly the flavor of the month as far as they're concerned. For the Batswana, snakes are mixed up in witchcraft and all. The locals don't want to have anything to do with them. The poor students on the other hand, didn't have a choice. A student had to unlock the door at each locker, so the deputy could throw it open.

"It was quite a show. Opening each door, the deputy screamed like a bloody kamikaze. We stood by with big sticks and burlap sacks in case a snake came out. These cobras spit a mile, so the bag was our protection. Cover the snake and beat the crap out of it. The deputy was the only one enjoying himself."

As we stood talking, a donkey-drawn cart clattered past and we had to move to make way.

THE COBRA IN THE SAND was a genuine new experience and in some mysterious way it seemed to open my mind to new possibilities. For one thing, the cobra was real. Many of the anxieties causing me stress at the time had to do with nebulous problems that I couldn't really touch, or see, or feel. Like the concept of impermanence, for example. This snake, however, though it was dead, it was real. It was an immediate connection with reality and danger.

During our time in the village, I'd been playing mind tricks, reminding myself of all the wise things I'd read about impermanence. *Things fall apart and all things end . . . Life goes on . . . Nothing lasts forever and nothing remains the same.* My reminders probably didn't do any harm, but I couldn't tell that they did any good, either.

After the continual anxiety, the sight of a cobra made me feel engaged, as if I was a participant in something important. I began looking, and really seeing, the new forms of life that surrounded us. It was invigorating and added a dimension for me. The snake put things into perspective. Realizing that these lethal creatures were my neighbors gave me a life or death view of the world. My anxieties over trivial details shifted further down the list of my concerns.

Right away I started hearing more about venomous snakes.

The staffroom was long, and shadowy, and crowded with dark furniture. The chairs were heavy and straight backed, and stained a dark walnut. A few bench seats, placed near the walls, were padded with pillows of a somber brown.

The deputy, Mr. Ramasamy, often came there for needed moments of relaxation during the day. He was a small man, quick and dark skinned, and he liked to chat. When I first met him, he introduced himself as a French-speaking Hindu Tamil from Mauritius. I admired his ability with language and when he talked to me he used a bit of American slang.

Most mornings, Ramasamy came into the staffroom to smoke a cigarette. On one particular day, he sat down near me during the morning tea break, lit up, and said, a bit too casually, "I found a mamba last night."

"You found it? Where?" I asked.

"In my garden," he answered. He inhaled and released smoke slowly through his nostrils. Ramasamy's eyes were in constant motion that morning. It wasn't unusual for him to take in everything in the room from where he sat, but that morning, he seemed especially keyed up. Perhaps, on edge still, from seeing the mamba.

He and his wife lived in one of the houses near the school. "My wife and I came home about ten from a visit with friends in Francis-town . . . kids asleep in the back . . . and as soon as I drove in, I saw him in the headlights. A goddamned mamba! Saw the fucker with my own eyes! Huge! Slithering through the grass near the house. We sat there in the car and watched where it went. Then I went to get the night guard while my family stayed in the car. I came with the guard and my wife moved the car to help us find him in the head lights. Finally, the guard and me . . . we smashed him with our sticks."

Ramasamy got excited telling the story. He smoked rapidly, taking one draw after another on his cigarette. Then he lit up another. His cigarettes, with a kind of tobacco I'd never been around before, had an unusual heavy aroma. When he finished telling me about the mamba in his yard, he paused, smoked for a minute, then launched into another story about a mamba in Mauritius. That snake, he told me, was six inches in diameter and lived in a drain lined with tile in his yard.

My inner voice scoffed, a mamba *"six inches in diameter"* — *either he's trying to impress me, or he's talking about a python.* But I didn't say anything.

Ramasamy laughed and added, "I felt nervous being in my own yard . . . working in my garden. So, I used to watch it out of my window. The snake liked to lay out on a rock . . . soaking up the sunshine. I watched him and one day I found out where he lived. He had this hole in the yard . . . well hidden, but when I saw him crawl in, I put a rock over the opening."

Ramasamy had draped himself across two of the wooden chairs. His arm dangled over the back of one, smoke rising from his bad-smelling cigarette.

"That rock, I could hardly lift it," he said, showing me the size by holding his hands about a foot and a half apart. "The next day," he told me, "the rock was pushed to one side."

"He was too big and I could never get him. Finally, He and I made a pact. He stayed in the drain and only came out when we weren't in the yard. He never broke the pact. Whenever anybody was working in the garden, the snake would never show his face. In return, we let him alone and he killed all the rats that came anywhere near our yard." Ramasamy paused to take a drag on his cigarette. "I think he got some neighborhood dogs, too. But we didn't criticize him for that. Even a snake has to live. He did his part. I did mine. We got along."

His eyes darted around the room for a second, then paused and seemed to brighten. "Eventually, I put in for a transfer," he said. "When I moved out of that house, I walked over to his hole and waved goodbye to the opening." Ramasamy made a comical little bye-bye wave, the kind you'd give a child. He then said, "I told him 'It's all yours.'"

I listened to Ramasamy's stories in the staffroom with a naïve interest. I had no experience with poisonous snakes. All my life snakes had been characters in stories. As a child I'd seen comic book serpents coiled in a tree or on the ground. They represented an idea, like the serpent coiled in the tree of knowledge offering forbidden fruit — temptation. Even in comic books, snakes were fascinating. In the house I grew up in, a bronze image of a cobra — a candle holder from India — sat on a bookshelf in our living room. A family friend had given it to my mother. It rose from a coiled position, its intricately decorated hood spread wide. My mother told me it represented a mysterious life force.

I was a child when we talked about it and didn't understand what she meant. But it intrigued me, the paradox of a venomous serpent representing a force for life instead of death. Later, as an adult, I read a parable about a man who walks into a room and sees a rope coiled in the corner. Instantly, he thinks it's a snake. His mental picture of the world at that moment becomes his reality—adrenalin pumps, his mind races, and he experiences fear. His reactions are the same as if there were a real snake in the room, not just a coil of rope.

As a parable, of course, the story had a lesson. The man reacted without thinking — taken in by delusion.

TOWARDS THE END OF THE WEEK, Gen and I were both dragging and to make matters worse, cooking and washing dishes were slowed by a clogged drain. Water seemed to just sit in the kitchen sink. Bailing it out by hand was the only option. I told her I'd try to fix it on the weekend.

By Friday I was done in and there was no let up. I'd set aside time for grading essay books, but a school cleanup project intervened and I had to work with students mopping, sweeping, washing windows, and wiping furniture in my classroom.

Both of us arrived home late. I stayed outside watering plants in our vegetable garden, and was there when Gen called to me, complaining again about the sink. Along with everything else, the backup in the drain was too much for her. I fixed dinner that night and afterward, decided to look at the sink. I wasn't sure what to do about it and didn't have any tools, but I crawled underneath to see if I could locate the problem. The elbow consisted of a rubber sleeve held on by a clamp and I was able to loosen it with my fingers. The sleeve was flexible and I poured the contents into a pan. Then I tightened the clamp and turned on the tap. The sink filled up immediately.

The blockage had to be in the pipe outdoors, I decided. The drain extended through the wall of the house and made a right angle bend down the outer wall. The pipe ended about a foot above ground over a drain cover. Outdoor light was fading and I needed a flashlight in order to see what I was doing. The first thing I did was to unscrew an inspection cap located near the ninety degree bend. The cap popped off as if it was under pressure and then I discovered the cause of the back-up. Through the round hole, I saw the scaly skin of an animal stuck in the pipe, pinkish in color with a black dotted diamond pattern. Immediately, I thought of the snake I'd seen on the dusty road and Tim's words, *"these cobras spit a mile."*

I went in the house to tell Gen and she wanted to see for herself. Then, both of us wanted to look again, just to make sure. That moment was our pinnacle of mutual hysteria, both of us giggling nervously.

Dishes were still unwashed when we went to bed, and all night I dreamed of snakes. In my dreams, I worked at various ways of dislodging a venomous serpent from our plumbing, while reptiles crawled through every room of the house — snakes in the pipes and in the yard.

In the morning, I dragged myself out to accomplish the task that must be done. Facing death, I didn't want to worry about breakfast. My tool for dislodging the serpent in the pipe was a wire clothes hanger that I'd straightened and bent into a hook at one end. Walking around to the side of the house, I unscrewed the inspection cap one more time.

The pink flesh bulged out of the hole as I worked the stiff wire in between the side of the pipe and the animal's skin until I felt the creature starting to move. My feet were placed a few inches from the grill where the pipe emptied into the drain field. Suddenly, I felt the thing come free. With a sucking sound, it slid down the pipe and I heard it splat near my feet. I jumped back and then saw the body on the grill below.

A huge bullfrog lay at my feet.

The poor creature had somehow crawled up the pipe and got stuck in the ninety degree bend. For two days it had swallowed everything we'd tried to pour down the drain and now, it was impossibly bloated.

The whole episode was an embarrassment and reminded me of the story about the man and the coil of rope. The man taken in by ignorance and delusion — that was me — temporarily unhinged.

I HAD BEEN TEACHING at the secondary school for nearly six months and the term was nearing an end. The weather was changing, too. We were entering the cool season and the earth was making a gradual change to allow nature to perform its balancing act.

In my garden, it was life and death. Working in the garden had helped me deal with a lot of the stress I'd felt when we arrived, and garden tasks seemed to help in making the kind of shift I needed to accept change and transience. But now, I was watching my plants shrivel. The tomatoes and eggplants had already yielded three crops of bright red and purple vegetables, but they quit producing.

We were settled in our new house, and on the weekends I'd become used to taking my morning cup of tea outdoors to watch the sunrise across the road. A sparse grove of thorn trees grew there, and some mornings, as the sun rose orange in the east, the light silhouetted a pair of donkeys grazing on the razor sharp grass under the trees. Evenings, Gen and I sat on our porch with a glass of juice or a beer. I'd planted a hibiscus bush near the porch and each day the shrub shed the previous day's blooms. In the morning, dry flowers lay scattered under the plant and new buds began to open. By late afternoon, we had glorious red blossoms that were always fresh.

The mornings were chilly, but by noon the air would be a moderate temperature. Eighty degrees Fahrenheit felt like the new moderate in the desert. Many days in the early morning, a steady wind blew from the south — our neighbors called the wind "an Antarctic chill." The cooler weather made me think of home in the U.S. where it would be spring and flowers would be blooming after a long, brown season.

I was wrapping up work with my classes in preparation for my transfer from the junior secondary school to the Tonota College of Education, and was feeling pressed to complete everything. At the same time, I was beginning to feel pangs of loss knowing I'd miss the teachers and the students at the school. I was keenly aware of how much I appreciated my time there.

Other teachers were also finishing work with their classes and everyone seemed to be slowing down. Conversations often took place in the staffroom during tea break or an open period when I happened to be sitting at one of the long mahogany tables going through my unending stack of student essay books. We had long discussions about personal events or news someone heard on the BBC the night before. I was always happy to put down my red pencil, change my posture, and chatter. I'd talk with anyone who had a few minutes and I relished the interruptions.

One of the teachers who was frequently in the staffroom was Mma Katata. She was unusual in that she preferred to be called by her first name, Gurley. Chatting in the staffroom was a big part of her social life. She lived in teacher housing and, with no means of transportation, she appeared to live in isolation, responsible for the support of her child. If her child was sick, she missed class.

Gurley took meticulous care of her appearance, her shoulder length black hair was always neatly combed. Her clothes, mostly homemade, were straight out of the pages of fashion magazines. Often, she had a colorful scarf draped around her neck and shoulders. Her reddish mahogany skin had a special glow — evidently, the result of creams and moisturizers.

The father of Gurley's infant son taught in a village near the Zambian border and he visited her and the baby on weekends. Since teachers in Botswana often couldn't afford automobiles, he traveled by hitching a ride or taking one of the aged buses that traveled the national highways belching black smoke, rolling on precariously balding tires. The buses broke down frequently, and most people tried to avoid them if they possibly could.

Gurley said that her fiancé was trying very hard to be transferred to Tonota. The weekends he didn't visit her, he went to Gaborone, to make his case to the clerks at the Ministry.

Many afternoons, I found myself listening to Gurley in the staffroom. She sat in one of the comfortable, padded chairs, looking elegant in a patterned, rust-colored dress with a high collar, a bright scarf over her shoulders. Often, as she talked she hand sewed a piece of fabric, a seam or a hem for another dress. As she carefully stitched, she described her frustration about the fact that her fiancé had not yet been able to work out a transfer and spoke of his adventures as he traveled on the notoriously bad buses or about the drivers he hitched rides with who turned out to be reckless and or drunk.

"I want him to transfer," Gurley would say to those of us seated around the room, talking to whomever wanted to listen. "If he works in Tonota, we can get married. But the Ministry is so reluctant. I don't know why they delay."

My last week at the school, Gurley did not show up for work on Monday. By afternoon, through quiet whispers, news traveled among the staff about her fiancé. On a trip to Gaborone to plead for his transfer, he had hitched a ride and, sitting in the back of a pick-up truck as it ran off the road, he was killed.

She didn't come to work on Tuesday, either.

That was the same morning a young girl went into the lavatory and after she sat down, she happened to notice a puff adder coiled in the corner of the stall a few feet from her legs.

I overheard teachers telling the story of the girl and the snake that day in the staffroom, their laughter echoing off the concrete walls as they described her running out of the stall. In the dying days of the school term, it was told and retold, gradually embellished with more detail — how she screamed — how she had left her underwear behind.

It became the story of the week — repeated over and over — with the same narrators, same audience, and each time, the same stunned laughter.

Friday, I left the school, still in disbelief, but at the same time, with a realization that I couldn't live in Africa with the same innocence I took for granted in North America. The life I had lived, sheltered from random danger and capricious death, was over. The week's events caused me to see things I'd never thought about seriously. Do I ever know what's going to happen tomorrow? Do my plans ever turn out the way I envisioned? Outcomes are a vague approximation, at best, when I really take the time to examine them. As events unfold, everything feels accidental, the future unpredictable.

THE DAY THE TERM ENDED, I spent an afternoon writing letters, trying to catch up on correspondence to friends in the U.S. That evening, Gen and I sat outdoors on our front porch sharing a beer and watching the sunset. The evening was quite comfortable and we sat in silence as the western sky turned deep red, and darkness closed in like a huge eyelid, gradually enveloping the entire sky.

It was nearly a year ago that we had packed our belongings into the basement of our house, locked the door, and walked away. I recalled telling Gen that I needed a change, a fresh start. At the time I had no idea what I really needed, but we had plane tickets for Thailand where we worked until the Peace Corps got in touch with us.

She and I had been in this village six months. Gen, whose career had been in business, was now teaching home-ec. For those six months, I'd been a middle school teacher, a big change from working at a college. A year ago, would I have been able to predict where I'd be the following year?

One thing I was sure of. I didn't know I'd be telling my friends, in letters home, how content I felt, living in Africa.

# Tim and the Five-Paragraph Essay

IT WAS EARLY MONDAY MORNING, the beginning of my second week of walking to work, and as I was hurrying along the shoulder of the main road of the village, the sun began to rise in the east.

Halfway through my nine-kilometer walk, the sun was still low on the horizon, but I had already worked up a sweat, when I was surprised to hear a voice say, "Can I give you a lift, mate?"

A dirty-gray Toyota sedan had just pulled to a stop and the window was down.

"Thanks." I opened the door and as I climbed in my foot accidentally kicked an empty beer can — a blue Foster's Lager — causing it to rattle across the floor. The driver smiled. We introduced ourselves — his name was Tim — and then we realized that we taught at the same school.

"I'm wiped," he said. "Until an hour ago, I was watching the Super Bowl in town. Me and a couple of your countrymen. A glorious waste of time." He went on to describe how, just as one of the teams lined up to kick a field goal that would decide the game, the

TV connection was lost. He gave me a wry smile. "In about a week, we'll know who won."

I'd been in southern Africa for only two months, but I knew what he was saying. We had a laugh. It wasn't just about the Super Bowl. We were in a part of the world where disconnections prevailed between local cultures and events in the rest of the world. On this dusty road, the disconnection cemented a kind of bond between us.

My wife and I had been delivered to the village about a week ago and didn't yet have a permanent living arrangement, and my teaching assignment was temporary, as well. I was scheduled to teach at the college of education in a few months. But until then, Tim and I would both be teaching English at the secondary school.

He was thirty-two, about twenty years younger than me. His boyish face with its expression of childlike innocence didn't seem to fit his broad-shouldered physique. He was wearing an Oakland Raiders cap, though as I got to know him, I learned that his usual style included a wide-brimmed fedora with a couple of colorful bird feathers in the brim.

Our school required teachers to follow a dress code, but because of the heat, I always went without a compulsory jacket. Tim followed the rules to the letter. He wore his brown herringbone sport coat and greasy necktie even on the hottest days.

As I was getting to know him, I commented that his Australian accent seemed pretty mild. "When I came here," he replied, "no one could understand me. I had to change my ways and now I sound like a bloody Pom." I wasn't sure what a Pom was, but I guessed it meant an Englishman.

He'd grown up in Brisbane, which happened to be about the same southern latitude as the part of Botswana where we worked. The youngest in a family of six boys, Tim's mother died when he was ten. His father followed a few years later.

"Ever read *Lord of the Flies*?" Tim asked me.

I told him I had.

"Then you know something about the family I grew up in." For most of his youth, Tim had lived in an unstable and hostile environment. From the way he described his life, I could imagine a young boy who wanted order, fighting a world in which nothing lasted, using a constant state of rebellion as a strategy to survive. *How is a boy supposed to find meaning in life if nothing lasts? . . . If there's no certainty or even safety?*

I felt that I could understand Tim because my father died during my adolescence. It's a past that refuses to go away. I could understand how the loss of a parent leaves a boy feeling betrayed. And how everything seems temporary. What endures? Nothing. Nothing is certain and every leaving feels like a death. A kid in that position grows up with a lot of anger.

In his search for order, Tim had become a dedicated teacher and put a lot of energy into his work. Two afternoons a week when classes were over, he and I helped the coach with the track team. On the other days, Tim and I organized an after-school English language club. We gathered reading material for students who participated, and during the meetings, had small groups conversing in English.

Tim became my mentor, of sorts, while I tried to get used to the Cambridge style of education in Botswana's secondary schools. The Cambridge tests were a series of make or break exams written, scheduled, and marked in England. They loomed over the school year. Had any of the test makers ever been to Botswana? I doubted it. Yet students had to pass the tests in order to move on to the next level.

In the evenings, after both our work days were over, I heard stories from my wife about the Cambridge home-ec curriculum in which girls were tested on their knowledge of how to polish silver or clean crystal. Skills completely irrelevant to the life of students in the Kalahari Desert. Most of our students lived in round mud huts with thatched roofs. Families didn't have electricity. Children didn't have toys.

*Crystal? Silver? Give me a break.*

English classes were presented with a series of structured forms that pupils were supposed to internalize: business letters, letters of application for a job, and the five-paragraph essay. None of it stimulated creative juices for these young adolescent writers. The educational system's irrelevance to the real life of the students seemed like a betrayal. But if I introduced something I thought would add interest, I met with resistance. Students would say to me, "Sir, this will not help us on the exams."

The more I learned about the curriculum, the stronger my belief that the rules and exams were overly rigid and dry. One day I said to Tim, "This is a system that guarantees failure."

There was a lot that Tim didn't know about life, but he knew everything there was to know about the Cambridge System. All of his schooling in Australia and his eight years of teaching in Botswana had been within that system.

Tim's response to my questions and complaints was always good natured. "No worries, John-O," he'd say, his eyes twinkling with pretended cynicism. "You teach 'em the rules, give 'em lots of repetition, and we're all in paradise."

His jokey style was an act. Tim was a believer. He didn't mind if it was a hangover from the days of colonialism. Cambridge was synonymous with education for him. It had saved his life.

Tim told me about his early years. "My life was in a tailspin," he said.

We were sitting at one of the thick, hardwood tables in the teacher's room and I became intrigued by what he was telling me. Suddenly, I understood him. I realized that all of his stories were the perfect model of a five-paragraph essay.

The five-paragraph essay was the only way Tim knew to unlock the secrets of an irrational world. He described his chaotic life in those early days in well organized, clear steps — including rules and lots of repetition. In that essay form the introductory paragraph might include a thesis or statement of need. In the next three paragraphs, as every school child learns, the writer develops the argument and then, according to the rules, the last paragraph states a summary of the ideas presented and the conclusion.

In the days shortly after Tim arrived in Botswana, his thesis had been "The Importance of Meeting Needs." He felt his needs strongly. On his days of rage, need hit him in the face and left him struggling. His proposed solution — developing his argument — had two parts: First, get drunk, and second, seduce every woman teacher in the school where he worked. The conclusion was not always a pretty sight since it involved a huge hangover.

Then, Tim met Shavala, a statuesque Motswana woman whose beautiful dark skin was the color of deep mahogany. She often wore a flowered wrap-around skirt and a blouse of bright orange that showed lots of cleavage. Heads turned when Shavala entered a room.

"She got preggers," Tim told me, "so I married her." Eventually, Shavala gave birth to a baby girl named Shanti.

The Cambridge System had not prepared Tim for anything like Shanti. She was a total surprise. He discovered, to his delight, that he adored the child. He sobered up and moved to his wife's matrilineal village.

Shanti was about two years of age at the time I got to know Tim. I used to see them together on Saturdays when my wife and I went to town for groceries. He'd be holding the child's hand or carrying her in his arms. Shanti seemed to reconnect all the broken bonds in Tim's life. With his daughter, he was the picture of domesticity. Totally content and attentive.

Once when we were talking, Tim told me that he'd taken Shavala and Shanti to Brisbane to meet his brothers the previous year during the August school break.

"How did that go?" I asked.

"So-so," he said. "Taking an African woman to Australia is chancy. My brothers were not thrilled. But they're a buncha *ockas*. They see dark skin and throw a wobbly."

I didn't know what he was talking about.

"Ockas," he said. "You would say rednecks." He smiled at me sheepishly, looked away, and then he added, "In Brisbane, a dark-skinned, African woman is not exactly the favorite flavor of the month."

Shavala was a strong, dignified woman, in a line of women who headed their tribal group. I never had a chance to ask her about the trip to Australia. I did wonder, however, how a proud woman like her had reacted to the kind of insults she undoubtedly experienced.

One afternoon, Tim invited me out to his wife's village.

Set on a hillside about thirty minutes from school, acacia thorn trees dotted the sloping landscape and shaded the huts. There was no sign of Shavala or Shanti when we arrived, but he introduced me to the head woman of the village, who happened to be Shavala's grandmother. An elderly woman, her dress hung loosely over her slight figure. Her moon-shaped face was weathered, her skin the color of dark coffee, and her hair wrapped with a white scarf.

She greeted Tim graciously with a broad smile and he introduced us. I wanted to be friendly, of course, so I showed off my Peace Corps language training by greeting her in Setswana, the national language. "Dumela, Mma!" I said, my knees bent slightly to show respect, "*O tsogile jang . . ..*" The full traditional greeting is a long phrase, but I wasn't able to finish because I saw by the glare in her eyes that something was wrong. The look she gave me suggested that a baboon had just entered her courtyard.

I stopped and Tim said something to her in a language I didn't recognize. It was only then that I realized Setswana was not her language. I should have known. She was a member of one of the minority tribal groups and some of them bear resentments toward the Tswana, and they're reluctant to speak the language.

Despite the awkwardness of the moment, her anger was short-lived. She simply gestured for me to sit down, extending the kindness one shows a less intelligent person. To sit with her was to sit in silence for however long she wanted to be with you. In a well-maintained mud-daub courtyard beside her thatch-roofed hut, we sat for fifteen minutes.

Afterward, Tim showed me the village. He had an obvious pride in conducting the tour. "We're all in paradise," he said more than once on our brief rounds. By this time it was a familiar phrase of his. I'd heard him use it for all kinds of situations. As we walked I noticed that we didn't see any other men. That didn't seem too unusual at the time, because in Botswana, a lot of men left to labor in South Africa or work in a farm plot outside the boundaries of the village. Later, however, I did begin to wonder how Tim fit into a village where there were only women and children.

In the weeks following my visit to his wife's village, when I saw him with his daughter, I began to sense a fantasy playing out in his mind. He wanted a family for his daughter, a perfect family, full of love and nurturing, with time to play and care for her. A conventional Westerner's dream. Tim was fantasizing the kind of family he had never experienced and he understood very little about the family he was trying to fit himself into.

But he had turned his life around. By now, he was working on a new five-paragraph essay on self-improvement. At school, he talked about his family and their village. I came to understand that the exotic nature of the life was rewarding — sitting with elders in a ritual moment, speaking to his neighbors in a language he hadn't known until he came to Africa.

Yet, Tim was always an outsider.

Marriage in southern Africa is governed by tradition. It's a union of two families, often formed as an alliance. The process of marriage begins with negotiations between the two families. Cattle are exchanged because the price of a bride is set on the basis of cattle. When an expat like Tim, enters the negotiations as a person without cattle, the result is he is a person with little status.

THE LAST WEEK of the school term, Tim got the news he was being transferred. He had not been consulted about the transfer and it was a shock — it seemed to come from out of the blue. On Monday, I heard him on the office telephone speaking angrily with someone at the Ministry.

"How could this happen?" I heard him ask the person on the other end of the line.

What made it particularly difficult to understand was that his wife's cousin in the Ministry of Education had initiated the transfer.

By midweek, Tim was silent and morose. Without warning, he was being transferred to a school a hundred kilometers south. His wife's cousin was in charge of the paperwork at the Ministry, and though Tim wouldn't talk about it to me, there was an obvious implication that Shavala may have been pulling the strings.

Late Friday afternoon, when I saw Tim come into the staffroom, his eyes were bloodshot. He had opened the heavy mahogany door and entered recklessly drunk. Walking unsteadily, he was carrying a four-foot pole. I was talking to another teacher at the time, but the Africans in the room immediately saw what was happening. They gathered the papers they'd been grading and rushed out the back door with their arms full of student essays and exams.

After the room cleared, Tim began pounding a table top with his stick. When I saw the way he looked at me, I wondered about my decision to stay behind.

Nevertheless, above the banging I asked, "Are you going to transfer, after all?"

He glowered and swept a table with his pole, scattering papers and knocking a coffee cup to the floor.

"When will you be leaving?" I asked. "Is there anything I can do to help?" I wanted him to talk . . . to spill it.

He raised the pole over his head and sent it crashing onto the table's varnished surface.

Tim ignored everything I said.

"Fags," he screamed. "Bloody bunch-a sods." His face was red and the tears began to flow. He was not going to talk to me and wasn't going to hurt anybody or himself, so I backed out of the room. The explosion of the pole against the table top echoed from the cement walls of the nearly-empty staff room. Tim was setting out to destroy the place, but the concrete walls and heavily-built furniture were impervious. I reached the doorway and left.

"Bloody sods!" he roared as I walked out the door.

A few days remained before the end of term. During that time, I felt anger rising in my chest before I realized I was in grief. Tim was my friend and he was leaving.

I caught him in the staffroom on the last day of the term. We promised to stay in touch, but it would be our last conversation.

The next term each of us wrote one letter to the other, and after that, I didn't hear from him again.

## Diamonds

I HAD MY FIRST GLIMPSE of the new teacher a few days after the beginning of the second term during morning assembly. The entire student body and all of the teachers were gathered on the school grounds under the flagpole. As hymns were sung, the flag of Botswana swayed tentatively in a slight breeze, then, after a Bible reading and recitation of the Lord's Prayer, it was time for announcements. The headmaster reported that some keys had been found. He held up his hand, a key ring dangling from his index finger. Then the deputy headmaster stepped forward and delivered a tirade about sweets wrappers cluttering the school grounds. At the end, the headmaster said in a matter-of-fact tone of voice, almost as an afterthought, "The new teacher has arrived."

That was Mr. Mothumo's introduction to 400 students. I looked across the school grounds and saw him standing near the door of the administration building amongst a group of teachers. About six feet tall, dark-skinned, he was wearing a straw-colored safari suit. I expected to see him step forward, perhaps hold up his hand in a wave of greeting, or maybe smile and nod to acknowledge, *I am pleased to meet you . . .. I am looking forward to being a teacher in this magnificent school . . .. We are going to have great times together.*

Mothumo didn't do that. Instead, as the curious eyes of 400 students turned to see who this new teacher was, he melted into the wall of the building.

For several seconds, he leaned further into the shadow of the doorway and seemed to shrink. There was no doubt in my mind Mothumo was deliberately trying to make himself invisible, and he nearly succeeded. Before my eyes, he became smaller and nearly disappeared completely into the shadows. I'd never seen anything like it.

Later that day, I walked through the staff room between classes and met Mothumo. He was sprawled across a cushioned seat meant for two people, and his dark skin glowed like polished ebony and his face seemed to have a permanent expression of surprise and fear. There was no way I could sit down next to him without becoming overly intimate, so I bent slightly, introduced myself and extended my hand.

In the U.S., when I shake a man's hand, I sometimes expect a show of strength. Some men communicate firmness. Others get competitive and squeeze until it hurts. But the hand Mothumo held out in response to my gesture was like soft butter. Warm and liquid.

In that first meeting, we spoke only briefly. There was warmth in his tone and his English was fluent, but his accent, with its elongated vowels and thickly rolled r's, made it difficult for me to understand him initially.

Mothumo moved into a house on the school grounds and became a magnet for the mothering impulses of several women. I could tell life was getting better for him when I saw him in the staffroom comfortably sprawled across the two-person padded seat during tea break, while one woman fixed his tea and another buttered bread for him.

I knew we'd eventually get our chance to have a real conversation. I'd begun coordinating all the teaching of English in the school, and sooner or later Mothumo would need supplies or answers to questions.

A few days after his arrival he did come to see me with a request for answer sheets to use in grading a standardized test. I found the answer sheets he needed in a storage closet and we sat down at a table in the staffroom.

He'd been out of college for only one term, he told me.

I asked how he was getting along with his class at the school.

"I see everything in reverse. It's so interesting. I can see myself in those children. I remember how it was in school. We had to be on time. We had to speak English. *Aiyy!*" He gave a falsetto yip. "A new language."

Mothumo glanced at the answer sheets he held in his hand and began to tell me about his transfer from the other school, his first teaching assignment. He needed the answer sheets, because he was marking papers from his previous school.

"I received a letter from the Ministry the last week of the term," Mothumo told me. "After the beginning of the new term, a truck came around to collect me and my things. I couldn't mark papers after I got my transfer letter. Aiyy!" Again, he punctuated his words with his falsetto yip. "When I got the letter I was so shocked. I had made friends. I had gotten to know my students. I felt so good about knowing the children in my classes and we were getting to the point where I was really helping them to learn. Aiyy!" His yip echoed off the concrete walls in the staff room. "Then I get that letter. I couldn't do anything. I went into my headmaster's office and cried. I cried for a week. I cried when I said goodbye to my students. My headmaster said I could postpone marking their term tests and do it later when I felt better."

All his talk about crying puzzled me, but I thought he might be exaggerating. As we sat together and talked, I kept thinking back to the morning of his introduction and the way he almost disappeared on the school grounds. He didn't meet my expectations that day. Of course, my expectations had been honed in the U.S. I would've considered it a sign of good manners to wave to the student body during his introduction and show some sign of outward enthusiasm. But judging from the way the women on the staff treated him, his way of being seemed to be an indication of good moral character.

I had seen the same kind of behavior almost on a daily basis. For many of the students, there was always a tension between the desire to be recognized and the wish to not stand out in any way. It puzzled me at times and made me wonder if there was an ethic to disappear in the village culture.

I had a student in my class who behaved in a similar way. He was named Goabaone and for him, even recognition in class by the teacher meant being noticed and giving up the comfort of the group. Whenever I asked a question during a class discussion, Goabaone's hand shot up, always the first in the air. His face eager, waving his arm in a way that said I have the answer, call on me. But when I called his name, a complete change took place in his behavior — excitement was transformed into docility. The hand he had waved excitedly in the air suddenly went to his forehead to cover his face as if he wanted to disappear behind his hand. While I waited with the rest of the class, a new expression came over him, eyes downcast, vacant. I had to repeat the question and wait. During the long silence that followed, he seemed to be trying his best to become invisible. Eventually, he answered in a barely audible voice. I then told him, "Say it so we can hear." It took two or three more tries before he provided a response.

His name, Goabaone, was pronounced wha-bah-Onay, and meant "God is the one who gives" in Setswana. I always wondered about the name. *Was that a reflection of parental gratitude? Does it have to do with karma? Fatalism or determinism?* His name probably had more to do with an attitude I'd seen expressed by a hand gesture used by people in the village. Sometimes, if a man or woman was asked a question they couldn't answer, they'd throw a hand in the air, palm outward — a gesture of helplessness — *who knows?* I'd seen men use the gesture if something went wrong, as if to say "it's out of my control!"

Perhaps his name had nothing to do with gratitude, karma, fatalism, or determinism. Possibly, after his birth, his parents threw their hands in the air to imply, this is out of my control.

Goabaone — I called him GB in class — showed up every Monday with his secondary school uniform — the light blue shirt and navy blue trousers — neatly washed and pressed. By Friday, after herding goats all week after school, his uniform was covered with dust and fur, and smelled like a goat kraal.

When I started calling him GB, in his quiet, undemonstrative way, he seemed to enjoy the new nickname.

GB was like a lot of the boys for whom the village was their corner of the world, where they developed their views about life. The village was a protective place that provided security, stability, and a place where one could disappear.

I taught at the secondary school for six months. Goabaone sat in my class each day dreaming, staring into the thorn trees outside the classroom window, a young boy with no particular ambition to do anything but herd goats. Maybe later, he'd think about doing the kind of work his male relatives did, toiling in the diamond mines or plowing a subsistence farm plot. In many ways, he reminded me of the way I was at his age. As a kid, I'd been a day dreamer, too. As far as my teachers were concerned, I was going nowhere and had no ambition beyond delivering newspapers to neighbors' porches.

During the times when the class worked on a writing assignment, I moved around the room to give assistance, and often, I was aware of Goabaone's eyes following me. He would study me with his dark eyes until he became distracted by something out the window, and then, staring into the bushveld outside, I saw him fade off into a daydream.

He'd grown up without material belongings — no toys, no gadgets. One day, I realized he didn't have a pencil or pen to write with, so I lent him a ballpoint pen, which I had clipped into my shirt pocket. The only pens he'd ever had were basic plastic. The one I let him use had a chrome top with a clip and push button. For several minutes he studied the pen carefully, testing the push button, until I prodded him to begin writing his assignment.

Another day, I stopped at his desk to check on work assigned thirty minutes earlier and saw that his blue essay book was blank.

"GB," I said, "are you having trouble?"

He said nothing, but his serious expression implied, I am deep in thought. Almost immediately his attention shifted to my digital wrist watch. By this time I knew a gadget could hypnotize him. Against my better judgment, I gave him a demonstration of the features: time in Botswana, time in Seattle, stopwatch, and alarm. It was a mistake, because the alarm was a happy tune that distracted the rest of the class.

"We have only a few more minutes," I said. "Get cracking, GB." Without a smile, he began to write.

Every week GB and I had a conversation about missing work. A solemn ritual between the two of us, in which he did his best to let me know — mostly through his serious expression—that the act of turning in an assignment was not a simple matter. His answer to my question about a missing assignment was often, "At the lands." That was where he spent his weekends working on his family's farm plot. "All my books are on that side," he'd say. And, as he told me that, Goabaone would throw his hand in the air, palm outward to emphasize his point, *it's out of my control.*

I'd ask again the next day.

He assured me that the paper had been completed, but unfortunately, it was in his locker. The reason he could not turn it in was that his locker partner had the only key to the lock. That boy had gone home sick.

Eventually, I got most of his assignments, but I had the impression turning in an essay book was not the important issue for him. He wanted the opportunity to give me an explanation of why it was not in class this particular day. Then, expressing a village attitude, he wanted to explain that tomorrow will be just as good.

When it came to any kind of schedule, villagers took a creative stance. The time for a program or meeting might be announced for 9:00 a.m., but the typical villager's attitude was, *the meeting begins when I get there.*

If I tried to prod Goabaone in order to get an assignment, his response always implied, *this is a matter I take very seriously. The consequences are far too important to simply toss my essay book on top of a pile of assignments.*

During the term, I began to enjoy hearing about the adventures of GB's essay book and I looked forward to hearing where things stood with his assignments.

ON THE LAST DAY of the term, the headmaster made an announcement during the morning assembly. "Mr. Ashford is leaving us to lecture at Tonota College of Education."

Later that day, Mothumo spotted me in the staff room during tea break and seemed visibly shaken. "You are leaving?" he blurted out. Tears streamed down his cheeks. "Who will help me?"

His tears flustered me. What had I done that was so important? It puzzled me, how a man could lay out his emotions so plainly to another man. I pulled up a chair to talk with him, but I didn't know how to handle the situation — the tears on Mothumo's face, and other teachers milling around, eating, drinking tea, and chatting. I felt uncomfortable sitting there with a man in tears.

The message I'd received as a child was, "Don't cry. Men don't talk about their feelings." Memories flashed through my mind, of times when I'd felt emotion and became inarticulate. Times when I completely choked up.

One of the women brought tea for Mothumo that she set on the dark-stained arm of the chair where he sat. I noticed the graceful shape of her hands as she positioned the teacup and saucer. Then she placed a buttered roll on a napkin nearby. All the while, she wore an expression of extreme caring and tenderness. It was the way family members might treat one another, with affection and kindness. No one in the room was looking at him with disapproving glances.

Gradually, a change came over me and I began to see things differently. His tears and her gesture of helpfulness were open expressions of caring. The way things happen in a village between people who belong.

When it was time for me to return to my class, fresh tears welled up in Mothumo's eyes. "There are too many transfers," he said. "Everybody leaves."

TWO WEEKS BEFORE I LEFT the secondary school, I had the students in my class write letters to junior high students attending a school near Seattle. "Imagine you are talking to Americans who are your age," I said. "Tell them about your school. Tell them what it's like to grow up in a village in Africa. Tell them what you do after school."

The letters were written and sent off before I left to teach at Tonota College of Education.

A month or so after I had transferred, a bulky package was delivered to my college mailbox. It was the replies to my former students' Pen Pal letters, and I had an opportunity to browse through the responses from some of the eighth graders living in the United States. The letters came complete with photographs and artifacts. Some photos showed families sitting in a living room on overstuffed furniture — there were television sets, decorative clocks, and pictures on the walls. Other families posed in front of two-car garages or suburban split-level homes with cars, boats, or motorcycles in the background. Money, baseball trading cards, and posters of Michael Jordan also were enclosed.

I KNEW THAT not having a photograph to send with their return letters might keep my students from replying. They had few belongings, no material wealth, and certainly none of them owned a camera. And to have a photo taken in the nearest town would cost them the equivalent of one U.S. dollar — a very large amount. So when I hand carried the packet to the teacher who had taken my place, I said to her, "Tell the students that I will take their pictures."

They started to show up at my house the next day, and more arrived after school every day for a week. When they came, I offered to walk into the village to take a picture of them near their family compound. That meant traditional round mud huts and conical thatch roofs as a backdrop.

None of them wanted thatch roofs. As a background for their pictures they all wanted a Western-style house — my house in the teachers' compound for instance.

Most of the girls wanted to pose in dresses other than their school uniform, and several girls came more than once. They dressed in bright colored dresses, and brought a change of clothes. Girls ducked behind a bush to change from one outfit to another, then sat on my front porch and fixed each other's hair, combing Afros or re-doing a weave. All of the girls wanted several good pictures. One girl told me, "Maybe an American boy wants an African wife."

At the end of a week, every one of the students accepted my offer to take a photo of them except for Goabaone and I put the word out among the students that I wanted him to come and get his picture taken. The message came back from more than one student that he would not have his photograph taken. No one seemed to know the exact reason. One student suggested that he had no way to pay for it, but I wasn't asking students to pay.

I knew that, among villagers, some didn't like having their photograph taken in the belief that a picture carried a part of the person's soul. A photograph could be used as a source of witchcraft.

I had no luck trying to locate GB and despite reminders from classmates, he didn't show up at my house.

TWO MONTHS AFTER my transfer, the Tonota College of Education hosted a program that drew well over a thousand people to listen to a speech by the Minister of Education. Entertainment and a feast were promised.

At the college, in addition to teaching my classes, I had the responsibility for managing TV services. I did my best with the new job and managed to train students to do most of the camera work. However, when the Minister and his entourage came to the campus, I was supposed to assist the Minister's media crew — a bossy and demanding group. They wanted to borrow college equipment and I was sure that, once we loaned it, we wouldn't see it again. Therefore, I did as little as possible and, in fact, I wanted to disappear altogether.

As I stood in the courtyard that day making myself as inconspicuous as I could I spotted Goabaone standing with a group of his adolescent friends. I looked across the courtyard and recognized the sheen of his black skin, the close-cut, tightly curled hair, and the dark eyes that seemed permanently focused inward on his dream world. During the preliminary program of dancing and choral music, the boys craned and moved together like a flock of birds, constantly shifting their position to find a better vantage point.

Goabaone and his group of friends stood on a small square of campus lawn. I wanted to greet him and walked in their direction. His eyes were averted the whole time. As I approached, he gave no sign of recognition. Of course, he'd avoided me for two months by this time, why would there be any change now? Perhaps he really didn't see me, though it was possible he was too shy to show any reaction. And then, he might have considered it rude to greet me first, since a child his age should remain quiet until spoken to. Whatever the reason, by the time I approached him, I was sure he'd considered the possibilities and ramifications of each. Still, it was possible he didn't see me until I spoke.

I was no longer his teacher, but I wanted some acknowledgment that he'd received a Pen Pal letter. Most of the class had received responses to their letters. I wanted to assure him, in case he wanted a photo or an idea for another object to send with his reply.

That day he was wearing a khaki short-sleeved shirt and shorts, his school uniform from the primary grades, though he'd been out of primary school for two years. The shirt buttons pulled the fabric to the stretching point and the shorts didn't look very comfortable either, but his family couldn't afford to throw away good clothes.

Approaching him, I said, "Goabaone, do you think you can visit the college and not greet me?" I affected a certain gruffness intending to elicit a smile. Instead, he shot a serious glance in my direction. His black eyes flitted toward me for a second. Then, with his eyes focused on the ground, he extended his right hand and grasped his forearm with his left in a traditional show of respect.

We clasped hands and I expected him to break away to rejoin his friends. To my surprise, however, he maintained contact. Holding my hand, he looked away, and said something softly that I didn't understand. He wouldn't look directly at my face.

"I couldn't hear, Goabaone. What did you say?"

"I got a letter."

"You got a letter . . . from America, you mean?"

"Yes."

Still maintaining contact, he held my hand with a firm grip letting me know he wanted my full attention. His eyes darted, gazing at the ground near our feet, then shifting to an object in the distance. There was something monumental bothering him — a weighty matter was on his mind.

"So, you received a letter. Did you answer?"

"No. I didn't reply them."

"Don't you think they'd like a reply?"

He continued to hold on. I felt his calloused hand, his grip tightened, and as he began to move, he pulled me along. Together we walked away from the crowd of boys. When we'd taken a few steps, he spoke in an earnest tone of voice, almost grave, but too soft for me to hear. I had to ask him to repeat.

"Diamonds. I am getting diamonds."

The words didn't make sense. I didn't understand how this fit into our conversation.

He had received a letter. Yes. He intended to answer. Yes.

"My uncle in the mines. Is bring me a diamond."

At that moment, someone touched my shoulder. I looked around — it was one of the men from the Minister's entourage. "A microphone has malfunctioned," he said. "We need a battery. Fully charged."

I'd been caught. "The Minister is getting ready to speak," the man said. It was an emergency. I'd have to let the man into the library and get him a replacement battery.

I still hadn't taken in what GB was trying to tell me. I turned to him and said, "Goabaone. Wait here. I'll be right back."

I dashed off to help the man and while I was on the errand, pictures began flashing in my mind of GB mailing an illegal diamond.

When I returned, Goabaone, had disappeared. I searched everywhere I could imagine for some sign of the group of boys. As a last resort, I wandered over to the soccer field where a crowd had gathered. Possibly, Goabaone and his friends headed that way. A match was taking place and spectators circled the pitch — a British term for a soccer field, but among the hundreds of people gathered there, I saw no sign of Goabaone, or the crowd of boys.

I did see one familiar face, however. Mothumo was standing on the cinder track along the sideline and I strolled over to greet him. He wore a cap with an olive drab kerchief that hung down the back of his neck to his shoulders. With that hat, he looked incongruously like a French Foreign Legionnaire. His dark mahogany corduroy jacket was a shade or two lighter than his skin. The smooth, glossy surface of his face reflected the afternoon sunlight.

I greeted him and asked, "Who's playing?"

"The college team and a first division side," he answered. "It's a practice match."

We were silent for a moment, watching players running headlong after the ball. Diving feet first, or jumping into a crowd for a header.

The eyes of every player on the ball, anticipating, and ready to go after it. Mothumo was focused intently on the action.

We stood on the track at the foot of a low rise. The field was pitted with small holes and a few patches of tough grass managed to survive on the rocky surface. Cattle from the college agriculture program had grazed on this field a month earlier.

I told Mothumo I hadn't watched a game for years. Not since my son was playing.

During a break in the action on the soccer field, I asked him about his background.

"I grew up in a small village about an hour to the north," he told me. Mothumo pointed to men on the field, telling me about their lives and I tried to form a picture of him running around a village with his peers — a band of small boys — like the group with Goabaone. At that moment the goalie for the visiting team ran for a ball — he ran with a distinct limp. "That man and I grew up next to each other. We went to the same schools, and I saw the game where he broke his leg. It never healed properly."

When I was ready to leave I said to Mothumo, "I came down here looking for a student from your school."

"Which one?" he asked.

"Goabaone. Know him?"

"Yes, I do know him." Mothumo nodded slowly, as if he was forming a picture of the boy in his mind. "I know him." Mothumo smiled. "He's a boy who will always live in the village, perhaps. Some children want to see the world. Test their wings. But I think if you and I visit in ten or twenty years, we will find Goabaone still here."

There was a brief silence and I saw an expression cross Mothumo's face. *What was it? Surprise? Fear?* I couldn't tell. Then he smiled. "On the other hand, ten years? He could be teaching school in that time." He gave a little laugh.

I told Mothumo that I'd been talking to him and we were interrupted. "I've been looking for him ever since."

"I haven't seen the boy," he said. "But those small boys . . . those boys move quickly. You might not catch up with them."

"That's what I'm afraid of. Anyway, I think I'll look to see if they're anywhere in the village." I waved, then hesitated and said, "By the way, there's going to be a staff party tonight. Why don't you come?" I hoped we might be able to continue our conversation. "You might enjoy it. There'll be music."

"Do you think it would be alright?" Mothumo asked.

"Yes, of course."

"But I am not a teacher on this side."

"You are my brother as a teacher and you can come as my guest. All of the teachers from the other side are welcome."

ABOUT 9:00 THAT NIGHT, the party was just getting underway, but the music was already too loud for my comfort. The off-white walls of the large staff room were made of concrete blocks and everything echoed. As I shouted my way through a conversation with another staff member, I saw a man in a French Foreign Legion hat and a dark brown corduroy jacket — Mothumo — entering the staff room through the open sliding glass door located in the corner of the room. The kerchief hanging from his cap concealed his face as he entered. I watched him slip along the wall of the room. He seemed like a much smaller version of the man I'd talked to at the football field.

Mothumo made a beeline for the beer cooler, reached in, turned, and then moved imperceptibly through the middle of the throng in the staff room. On his way out, a can of beer was tucked discretely under each arm. Mothumo passed through the same door he had entered and disappeared.

Watching Mothumo slip out of the staffroom, I thought about our conversation on the field and my errand earlier this afternoon. After I left Mothumo, I'd hurried to the edge of the campus to look out over the village.

I felt genuine fear for GB. It could be disastrous if he was caught mailing a diamond to America with a Pen Pal letter. It was illegal to send things like that through the mail. What if he wound up in prison because I'd assigned a letter. But who could know what the future held? There were so many possibilities. Ten thousand miles away, a middle school student might find a small rock tucked into a letter from Botswana. How would he react if he somehow discovered the rock was worth about four thousand dollars?

At the edge of the campus, I searched up and down the dusty road, but the boys were nowhere to be seen. Goabaone and his group of friends had disappeared into their familiar, protective village. I heard the clamor of bells that meant a flock of goats was somewhere nearby. A dozen eagles circled lazily overhead. Down the deeply rutted, dusty road two statuesque women carried water containers on their heads, chatting as they walked side-by-side, each with perfect posture. This road marked a line — a border — a world with different rules. Nothing had changed with the arrival of the Minister's entourage. No one had been affected by Pen Pal letters from America.

After a minute or so, I was no longer in panic mode. I wound up staring at the thatched roof houses clustered across the road from where I stood. As my mind cleared, it occurred to me, it was possible nothing would ever happen. Even if the uncle showed up with a diamond, what would it take to get Goabaone to put it in the mail?

Thinking these thoughts, I was ready to let go. Involuntarily my hand went into the air, *it's out of my control!*

**JULY 1991**

to

**JANUARY 1993**

## Outsider

I NEEDED TO MAKE A TELEPHONE CALL, and was sitting in the college lobby near the reception desk, waiting for one of the secretaries to help me, when a man scuffled in. I'd been at the college less than a month, didn't know many of the people on the staff, and I'd never seen this man. He was a short and broad-shouldered African, his clothes didn't quite fit, and his belly overhung his trousers, threatening to pop the lower buttons on his shirt. The top of his balding head was shiny, and he had a scruffy beard with wiry black hair poking out randomly. He was holding a piece of paper in his hand.

My negative first impression was that I was seeing a member of a motorcycle gang.

Dragging his heels with each step, he walked to the bulletin board, scanned it, then removed a thumbtack from one of the other notices, leaving it flapping. He then pinned up the paper in his hand, planting the thumbtack with his big thumb.

His errand apparently complete, he looked around the lobby and went back out through the double doors.

Bored waiting for a secretary to find time to help me, I got up from my chair and sauntered over to read the man's notice written in large letters with a blue felt pen:

FOR SALE

TOYOTA HATCHBACK

P5000

See Joseph K.

A mileage figure was written at the bottom, but I scarcely noticed. I was not in the market for a car and did not have 5000 *pula* ($480.00US).

A week after I'd seen the man in the lobby place the notice on the bulletin board, the entire teaching staff gathered in the lounge during staff tea. A hum of conversation filled the room when suddenly, unexpectedly, I heard clinking on the edge of a saucer with a teaspoon, the signal that someone wanted to make an announcement.

A voice boomed, "I have something to say."

It was the man I'd seen a week earlier. This day he wore a white shirt, its buttons straining against his pot belly. "Several days ago I posted a notice on the bulletin board," he began. "Since that time someone maliciously altered the notice. They changed the car's mileage and because of that apparently hostile act the car has not sold."

His announcement sounded like an accusation and seemed like a breach of etiquette. To my mind, this was a social time set aside for the teachers, not a time for accusations. But all conversations stopped, everybody listened, and instead of any sign of dismay, all the faces in the room were turned toward him with benign expressions, the man had everybody's full attention. When he finished, two or three additional announcements followed . . . a committee meeting in the afternoon . . . visitors arriving at the campus in the next few days.

THAT WAS MY introduction to Joseph.

He had been hired to establish an agriculture program at the college and the principal asked me to produce videotaped stories about the new program. During the next week Joseph and I made an appointment to discuss his project. He agreed to take me around and show me what he was doing in order to give me ideas for a story treatment.

On the agreed upon afternoon around two o'clock, I walked to his office, a temporary place located in a college warehouse on the extreme north side of the campus across the road from the cafeteria kitchen. Entering through the doorway, I passed palettes stacked with paper bags of cornmeal or mealies, sacks of sugar, and wooden boxes of fresh vegetables.

I found him at a desk in a closet-sized room that he shared with the cafeteria supervisor, a man named Mkwandla. Joseph was writing on a yellow pad when I arrived. He put down his pencil. "Ahh, you found me," he said smiling. "I'm well-hidden here."

"Crowded in here," I said. "I hope you and Mkwandla get along."

"Yes, we get along fine. He's never here. He maintains a desk and that's all."

I began the conversation by summarizing my needs for him. "I have to get ideas for visual ways of telling a story about your program," I said. "I want to see what you do and I'd like to participate in some of your agriculture classes. In other words, I want to watch you work. Eventually, I want pictures of students caring for animals, tending to the gardens, and actively taking part in classes." My task was to put ideas on videotape and I wanted to be in the spaces to get a sense of any lighting or technical problems I might run into.

Joseph smiled the entire time as I was talking. I had difficulty matching this friendly man with the one who had made that brusque, rude announcement about his car in the staff room. It surprised me that Joseph seemed open to everything I wanted. "Very good," he said. "Perhaps we can start today. I need to pay a visit to the cattle."

We left the office and walked along the edge of the fenced soccer field. Joseph was a powerfully built man and he walked awkwardly with a shuffling gait. I wondered as we walked, *why had he reminded me of a motorcycle gang member*? Then I remembered times when I had been traveling on highways back in the States, and motorcycle gangs, in their heavy leather boots, dragged their heels, as they paraded into a café.

The field we were on was the color of red sand and very dry. Workers had tried to get grass to grow, spraying the entire field — including chain-link fences — with a pasty, green slurry containing seeds and nutrients. But birds had consumed most of the seeds and goats had nibbled the hardened composition from the fences. As a consequence, the field had only patchy areas of grass.

The herd was small. At the west end of the field we found six cattle in a kraal browsing on bales of hay. The kraal was enclosed with a log fence. Water and feed was provided in troughs inside the fence.

"Later this week," Joseph told me, "there is supposed to be a truck bringing more animals. You might want to come over when they arrive."

I went again a few days later, after the truckload of cattle had been delivered at the campus. Joseph and I returned to the soccer field where some of the animals grazed on the playing surface.

"Fifteen cattle," he said. "They've had to survive a long truck ride. As you can see, some of them didn't do so well." One animal lay on the ground in an awkward position. "Look at this one," Joseph said. "The way it's curled up is going to hinder its efforts to breathe."

The animal appeared quite ill, possibly on the verge of death. Caked with dirt and manure, it appeared too weak to shift itself into another position. Joseph walked around the animal touching it gently, examining it as best he could. Then, I watched him lift the front end of the animal by the horns. After that, he walked around and lifted the hind end by the tail, using his great strength to shift the sick cow. Several times, he moved from the front end, then to the back, until the animal was lying in a more natural position. I was impressed with Joseph's strength. This was a full-grown cow, and, since the animal was not helping, Joseph was lifting dead weight.

After that day, Joseph and I rode into Francistown at least once a week and stopped to order cattle feed. We went into the feed store together and, invariably, the African woman behind the desk began directing her questions to me instead of Joseph. When that happened, I pointed to Joseph to let the woman know he was the man doing business.

Leaving the store, I asked, "Why was she talking to me?"

"She thinks you're the man in charge. I'm the helper. They just make assumptions."

I was surprised Joseph didn't feel more defensive about the situation.

As we worked together, I became more and more comfortable with Joseph. We spent time talking and I accompanied him regularly to get an idea of how his program functioned. Getting to know him allowed me to get beyond my negative first impressions. He and I always had a lot to talk about. He was an African man who could speak to me comfortably about African customs.

He was also a man of contradictions and paradoxes. Joseph spoke his own tribal language from Uganda, he spoke excellent English, though it was not his first language, and in the staff room I heard him speaking Swahili with instructors from Tanzania. Yet, despite the fact he'd lived and worked in Botswana for six years, he did not speak more than a few words of Setswana. In fact, most of his Setswana vocabulary, he learned from me.

Joseph was an outsider. He always seemed to be in a no man's land dealing with people he didn't belong with. As an agriculture instructor in a college that emphasized English, education, and academic topics he had to deal with faculty who knew they belonged. In order to survive with his dignity intact, Joseph had to make up the rules of how he was going to behave. There was always a question whether he belonged. He didn't know. The Ministry of Education didn't know. There were constant rumors that they were considering canceling his classes and his position.

Canceling Joseph's classes would have been a problem, however, for the college because all of the secondary schools in the country taught agriculture. Tonota College of Education would be without a way of training agriculture teachers for the many schools if the Ministry ended his program.

ONE DAY AS WE WERE TALKING, Joseph came up with an idea for a project to acquire a herd of dairy goats and build a shed to house them. I knew that USAID had grant funding available and I thought we might get grant money for the program.

Joseph jumped at the suggestion and immediately outlined a proposal. It would be a "model herd" of dairy goats. They would be fed and kept in a controlled enclosure. It would be a model for the farmers in the village who always let their Tswana goats roam freely to devastate the environment. A model herd of dairy goats would exemplify the nutritional benefit of having goats that provide milk. The milk produced at the college would be used in the kitchen. Both of us knew USAID was sure to like the environmental and the nutritional benefits of the project.

I wrote up the proposal based on Joseph's outline, submitted it, and within a couple of weeks we had a positive response.

ONCE WE HAD MONEY AVAILABLE, it became Joseph's job to find the goats.

One morning in the staff room he told me, "The only source is in South Africa. I found a farm and talked to the owner on the phone. I can't say I liked the man. He's an old Afrikaner. Conservative. Racist bastard. What bothers me is, if I show up by myself, will he deal with me? Then, I have to cross back into Botswana. What about the soldiers at the border? What are they going to do to me?"

Stories of extremely unfair treatment of Black Africans by South African soldiers were in the news every day. Joseph's fears were understandable. First, he would have to deal with a white farmer, and then what would happen when he tried to take the goats across the border?

"It would help if there was a white face in the truck," Joseph said.

I knew that traveling alone, Joseph would be vulnerable. Exaggerated pictures of violence flashed in my imagination. Listening to his description, I could imagine the fear he was experiencing. I wanted to help any way I could.

"I'll have a talk with the principal," I said. "See if I can get permission to go with you."

The next day I went into the principal's office and posed the question. "Joseph is going to South Africa to get dairy goats and he's nervous about the trip. We both wondered if it would be better if he and I went together."

The principal listened to me, then he looked up at the ceiling for a split second, and laughed. "Pah!" he said. "I can understand why he is afraid. However, dealing with South Africans is something Africans here have to learn to do. Joseph is an adult. He'll learn to handle himself. Going through the border, he'll deal with the South African Defense Force, and he'll learn what he has to learn. Everything will work out. But there is no way that I could justify sending two people and taking you away from your teaching duties for a week. In this part of the world, everyone has to deal with the South Africans."

I had no choice but to accept what he was saying. He knew better than I what Joseph had to deal with.

The time came for Joseph to go pick up a dozen dairy goats from the farm in South Africa. He and I went into town together to rent the truck. He'd leave the next morning.

IT WAS FRIDAY OF THE NEXT WEEK when Joseph returned, and on Monday morning I met him in the staff room and asked, "How did it go?"

"Surprisingly well," he said. "The gentleman was quite nice actually. He said he gets tired of dealing with government bureaucrats over the phone, so unless someone shows up in person he's not really interested in being friendly. He took the time to show me around. Besides his farm, he has quite a large cheese-making plant. But with the drought he's having a hard time making it go. He's selling off his dairy herd to bring in cash. Every winter, he and his wife go to the Netherlands. That's where he lives, actually. Turns out he's not Afrikaner. But a nice, liberal-minded Dutchman. Friendly. Just goes to show . . .."

I listened to him with interest. It seemed as if Joseph was describing another instance of being in a situation where he didn't fit in. But he made it work. He was constantly in his own "no man's land" and having to deal with people he didn't belong with . . . and making it happen.

"One thing surprised me," Joseph said. "In the South, every African I met spoke Afrikaans. There they were, black men. They looked like me. Africans speaking Afrikaans. Not a word of their own tribal language. I don't speak Afrikaans. I could speak English to the white man, the owner, but not the Africans. Can you imagine, . . . the Africans? I always assumed that we had a similar culture, but I couldn't talk to them! All the time I was there, the white man was the only person I could talk with."

FROM HIS EXPERIENCE with the dairy goats, Joseph learned some things that changed him. For one thing, he learned from his trip that not all South Africans were racist bastards, and there were other things, harder to put a finger on, that gave him a certain amount of self-confidence.

I could tell that he was more poised because he began spending a lot more time with the Africans on the staff than he did with me.

But even after I had worked with Joseph for months, his automobile sale continued to puzzle me. He had managed to sell his car a long time ago, but what was behind that strange accusation in the staff room that seemed so out of place? Probably, nobody in the room

106

really believed him, but how should he have acted? Should he have stifled his defensiveness? Should he have acted like a man bound by tradition and rules of behavior, confining and polite?

Maybe, as with his trip to South Africa, Joseph created a situation, sized up the other people involved, and then did what he had to do in order to get along.

## Sacrificial Beasts

THE SEASON HAD JUST CHANGED. Until a week earlier, an east wind blew steadily across the village, bringing dust storms and cold nights. During that spell, a shroud of red dust hung in the sky like a curtain and for days at a time visibility was limited by opaque clouds of sand. Then, very suddenly during the last weekend in August, the heat arrived.

The rapid shifts in weather made it feel as if natural laws were being broken. I'd been in the village for less than nine months; everything was still a first impression for me. I'd formed an idea of what the weather was like, but as soon as I felt I got to know a truth about how the elements behaved, the rules changed.

On a Saturday morning in early September, I was working in the red soil of my garden where life had regenerated, reproduced, and was restored. The garden plot amazed me — tomatoes and eggplants — crop after crop — even in the cool season. Except for my boom box blaring Radio Botswana's top hits, it was quiet that day in the teachers' housing compound at the college and it startled me when I heard the metallic clank of the goat bell that hung on my gate. I

109

looked up to see Peter striding across my yard. My neighbor across the street, fellow teacher, and head of the English department, Peter looked purposeful and focused. I studied his face trying to guess his errand. *College curriculum? . . . Social invitation?*

His brow furrowed, his mouth a firm straight line, Peter held his sharp chin and nose in the air. Being a Brit, Peter was never effusive, but he usually managed a business-like smile. Today, he looked utterly grim and said nothing until we stood face to face.

"Have you heard?" he asked.

I detected a slight tremor in his voice.

I shook my head, "Heard what?"

"Patrick . . .," he blurted, then struggled for words, his body shaking with the effort to speak. His knees seemed to buckle and I reached out to hold his arm until he was seated on the concrete step near my front door. He took several deep breaths before he could speak.

"Patrick died yesterday," Peter's chest heaved. "Very sudden. Such a shock."

Now I couldn't speak. The boom box pounded my ear drums while I pictured a wreck on the highway — a crumpled car, a pool of blood, and broken glass . . . Patrick on his bicycle . . . a drunken driver — the usual way Westerners die in Africa.

"In Francistown . . . he collapsed on the tennis court," Peter said, his voice sounding full of astonishment. "Can't get over it."

He held his head in his hands, elbows resting on his knees. "Healthy man. In the prime of his life." He closed his eyes. "How does it happen?" Then he shook his head in disbelief. "Just can't get over it."

Peter declined my offer of a glass of water. After a few minutes, his chest still heaving uncontrollably, he stood up and apologized for his display of emotion. "I'll be quite busy today," he said. "There are people to see."

He left and I went inside to turn off the boom box. I had enough noise in my head. Puzzling things had happened in the previous weeks, strange events. Omens, I'd been told, but since I had never experienced anything like that before, I had shrugged them off.

I sat in my yard stunned, sorting through the various incidents and warnings and trying to connect dots that, no doubt, shouldn't be connected. But, part of my mind was convinced I had prior knowledge. In those first moments of my confusion I wondered, *why don't I feel grief for Patrick?* Uncertainty was closer to what I felt, perhaps, even guilt.

Survivor's guilt. By some strange logic, I was sure that whatever happened to Patrick, who I had known for less than two months, was meant for me.

NEWS ABOUT PATRICK'S death spread through the campus and by three o'clock students gathered in the college assembly hall, forming a chorus. Two hundred voices calling and responding in minor harmonies, blanketing the campus. When one song ended a woman's piercing voice sang a first line to start the chorus on another. There was no part of the campus where the voices could not be heard — including at my house in the teachers' housing compound.

About half an hour after the singing began, I remembered I had an errand to run. I went inside to wash up, then walked the short distance to my office. On a sidewalk leading to the heart of campus, I turned the corner around a building and met a group of students, apparently on their way to join the larger group in the hall. One of the students stopped as soon as I came into her view. Her eyes at first registered recognition, as if something — a person's life, perhaps — had been restored. Her gaze seemed to say, *Aren't you dead?* Why are you here? A shift in her appearance occurred. She suddenly looked frozen and in shock. As we moved past one another, I felt her disappointment. I wasn't dead. My mind reeled. How many others had my face in their minds when they heard the news?

The encounter left me feeling weak in the knees. I took a second to look around to get my bearings. I was in a central courtyard planted with twelve-foot-tall poinsettias. When the students moved on, I studied the brilliant red blossoms and told myself, *I'm standing here looking at a courtyard full of red flowers. I must be alive.*

I returned from my errand, poured myself a glass of water, pulled out a chair from the kitchen, and resumed my position on the porch listening to the hymns coming from the hall.

My wife, Gen, was gone that day; she had returned to Seattle on a family emergency leave. Two weeks earlier, a time when nothing seemed to be going right — kitchen sink plugged up, electricity off most of the time, and water available only an hour a day — Gen received news that her mother's health had taken a turn for the worse. "Mercury must be in retrograde," she said in a wry tone of voice before she left. It was the only bit of astrology she ever referred to. Her all-purpose explanation for bad omens.

Alternating men's and women's voices echoed from the assembly hall all the way to the road. The music had a joyous quality and reminded me that in Africa, death always involves family and community. Because Patrick's family was in England, the students were performing the rites. Someone must grieve, a person should not have to go through the transition from life to death without people — lots of people — grieving the loss.

Sitting there, I thought about Patrick. I recalled how I'd checked my mailbox the previous Friday, and pulled a handful of messages from the slot in the staffroom, two of them addressed to Patrick Sherwood. At the time, I'd thought about finding Patrick and giving him his mail, but then remembered seeing him ride off on his bicycle. I told myself at the time I'd wait until Monday to give him the messages.

It had never ceased to puzzle me why his mail wound up in my box, but misdirection of our mail had become a regular occurrence. We had a ritual, Patrick and I. Handing each other mail, we'd exchange an ironic glance, but say nothing.

As I sipped from the glass of water, another image crossed my mind. An image of an owl. He fluttered his wings and looked directly at me. In my memory, sometimes the eyes were round and full of wonder. At other times, yellow eyes peered into my heart. "An omen" says a voice. "You should pay attention to this," says another.

The two messages addressed to Patrick still lay on a table inside my house and as I remembered the owl, I began to wonder, is it possible for omens to be directed to the wrong address?

IT WAS THE PREVIOUS JULY when Patrick and I both were introduced to college staff, and to other lecturers who had just returned from supervising student teachers at various area schools. Everyone gathered for morning tea in the staffroom where a film of the red dust coated the floor and furniture. Instructors, who had not seen some of their colleagues for months, stood holding teacups and saucers, chatting. When the deputy principal walked to the front of the room to begin the small ceremony, several people tinkled sugar spoons on their cups to get the attention of others.

Patrick and I stood side by side in the front of the room waiting to be introduced. Both of us had been assigned to work with second-year students and it was our first day of class. Patrick, four inches taller than me, was also twenty year's younger, clean shaven, and British. I had gray in my beard, a receding hairline, and was usually casual about my appearance. By coincidence, both of us had donned gray slacks and a blue blazer for the occasion.

The deputy principal, Mr. Chewe, a Zambian man, had the nearly black skin typical of central Africa. He stood with a heavy-lidded expression before the group, waiting for the clatter of spoons and the noise of conversations to quiet. Introductions were a formality since most of the teachers already knew us, but protocol required a ceremony and it was Mr. Chewe's job to pay attention to protocol. He was a pleasant, soft-spoken man. Though I found him a bit formal in his dealings, he was decent and willing to find common-sense solutions for thorny issues, as I'd discovered in the previous months when he helped me find housing on the college campus.

When he had everyone's attention, he said, "We have two new members of staff. I would like, at this time, to make introductions."

He turned to me and said, "First, please welcome Mr. Patrick Sherwood." Then he turned to Patrick. "I present you, Mr. John Ashford, the new lecturer."

Patrick and I looked at each other, both of us helpless to correct the situation without embarrassing Mr. Chewe.

At that moment, two teachers stepped forward. "No. This is Patrick," one said, pointing to the real Patrick. "And this is John Ashford," the other said.

Mr. Chewe's eyes darted between the two of us. "Well," he smiled diplomatically, "they do look very much alike. Do they not? Yes, I apologize."

He gave himself a second to recover and continued with a longer summary of our resumes. "Mr. Sherwood comes to us from the Ministry of Education in Malawi . . .." He described Patrick's background and turned to me, once again. "Isn't that correct?" Then he repeated the process, summarizing my experience and looked to Patrick for confirmation. By the time introductions were over, it was clear enough Mr. Chewe could not tell us apart.

We exchanged a glance, but said nothing at the time. Perhaps, we should have. Perhaps we should have decided then and there to distinguish ourselves outrageously. But that was not in our nature and the confusion of identity became both pervasive and persistent.

Events following that simple ceremony brought into question whether laws of cause and effect could be just as confused. Patrick and I regularly received each other's mail and telephone messages. The name clearly printed on the box seemed to make no difference and every day, students stopped me on campus to ask questions that had to do with Patrick's class, or wanting to make an appointment I knew was intended for Patrick. The same thing happened to him.

It was a source of tacit humor between us that we seemed indistinguishable to a large portion of the college community. Apparently,

Patrick and I were interchangeable parts or simply the same kind of part or animal to these people. Whether it be pencils or screws or light bulbs or goats in a flock — there may be slight variations — but there is no individual.

I DIDN'T KNOW PATRICK WELL. The few times we met socially were at Peter's house. One particular evening Gen and I joined Peter and his wife, Ellen, along with Patrick with his wife, Barbara, in a gathering on Peter's porch.

Peter's house was standard issue teacher housing in the compound, yet Peter and Ellen managed to create a bit of colonial elegance. The porch was covered by a shade net with the scent of frangipani blossoms from a nearby shrub. Smoke from a mosquito coil smoldered near the doorway. Peter's supply of liquor, bottles, and glasses rested on a low table as if placed there by an invisible servant.

The experience didn't mesh easily with my role as a Peace Corps Volunteer. At Peter's house, I felt out of place. Like the other men I wore a tie, but risking a breach of etiquette, I dispensed with the jacket — it was simply too hot.

We arrived a few minutes later than the invitation called for. Others were seated when we entered. I tried to make a joke about being late, but their silence indicated we had broken a strict English rule of punctuality.

Conversation at Peter's was always strictly segregated. Men's talk and women's talk. Ellen invited the women out to the yard where chairs had been placed between flowering shrubs. As I took a seat in the chair offered to me among the men on the porch, a glass of sherry materialized. I had no choice, though I always found it cloyingly sweet and distasteful. But this was apparently the hour when the English have a sherry.

Peter always placed the legs of his chair on the solid concrete slab that formed his porch. Maybe, the predictable solidity reminded him of England. As we settled into conversation, the two Englishmen leaned back, assuming a philosophical posture, each of them looking into the distance instead of at each other as they talked. In our group of three, Peter and Patrick did most of the talking. As an American, I was strictly an outsider. While they chatted about the news on the BBC, I sipped my sherry and listened.

Peter and Patrick had worked in various African countries for years, one of many connections between the two men that I didn't share. African language and customs were still a fascination to me since I had been in Africa for less than a year.

I entered the conversation by asking if Peter was aware that his next-door neighbor had found a puff adder in his living room. The previous Saturday, I watched the man's children burning the snake's corpse in the field next to the house. As they stoked the embers of the fire, I asked them questions. They told me their father was visiting the *n'goma* (witch doctor) to get advice on why the snake had visited in the first place.

Omens and witch doctors were integral parts of life in southern Africa, but taboo in conversation with the Brits and I knew immediately that I had spoken out of turn. Both of them sat in stunned silence. Peter gave me the kind of glance the British reserve for a colonial subject. Patrick wore a startled expression, as if he might be seeing me in a new light, reassessing his impression of my competence and intelligence.

I'd noticed anytime a matter of African culture came up in conversation, Peter exhibited impatience. His attitude seemed to be: We are the English. We're here to help people rise above all that.

The two of them quickly smoothed things over making a transition to topics more compatible with English sensibilities. Patrick made an announcement, "Barbara may be making a trip home soon."

"Oh, really," Peter said. "How nice."

"We'll decide within the next fortnight, but we think the boys ought to get a quality education. She needs to accompany them in order to get registered in a boarding school."

"They'll certainly get a superior education there," Peter said.

"Oh, no question," Patrick said. "None better."

Then the subject changed and they began talking about Margaret Thatcher. The mention of her name seemed to give them erotic pleasure, as if they were discussing a glamorous celebrity or movie star.

I went back to listening and Peter continued to provide generous refills of sherry.

During one lull in the conversation, I said, "I had an interesting thing happen this past Wednesday." I was feeling a warm glow by then. "I found an owl in my office. What a surprise that was."

Peter stammered, "Oh dear . . .," and seemed speechless for a moment. Patrick's face was a blank.

I began to notice a numb feeling in my nose. "Imagine my surprise. I came into my office that morning," I said, laughing a little too much, "and the damn bird was sitting in the corner. As soon as I entered, he pooped on the floor."

For a second, Peter's sharp face and eagle-beak nose directed a fierce gaze at me. Immediately, he poured more sherry into my glass, filling it to the brim — his nonverbal way of telling me, "Shut up!"

## II

ON THAT WEDNESDAY MORNING, I was carrying an armload of books to my office in the upper floor of the library. It was thirty minutes before my first class and my friend, Mr. Moepeng, the security man, had not yet arrived. I passed two women in blue cotton dresses as they were sweeping up the accumulation of red dust and large dead moths from the previous day. Shadi, her hair wrapped in a yellow bandana, held a mop in her left hand and waved a greeting.

Every morning I tried to say something in Setswana to Shadi in order to learn the language. That morning, I climbed the stairs rehearsing phrases in my mind for later use in conversation with her.

I unlocked my door, opened it, and across the room a large owl was perched on a metal rack intended for book displays. The eyes in the heart-shaped face were opened wide, giving me a hard, fearful look. All my practiced Setswana phrases evaporated.

*Am I really seeing what I think I'm seeing?*

Small birds occasionally came into the office through the open louvered windows and shooing them out was no big deal. But this owl was a foot-and-a-half tall. I couldn't believe a bird that big could squeeze through the two- or three-inch opening.

Owls are unusual. I'd never seen an African owl. Why would he want to come in here?

I watched him closely as I shut the door and set my books down on the desk. The metal rack rattled as he lifted his wings, gave a shudder, and splatted guano all over the floor. His white face jerked to one side, then the other — a panicked bird looking for a way to escape. Again, he spread his wings threateningly to impress me with his size.

I was impressed. I was also concerned about how to get the owl out of there. It would be a problem and I knew it immediately.

But still, it was fascinating to see this magnificent bird at such close range and I wanted to share my discovery with the women downstairs. Backing out the door, I composed a new phrase in my mind to tell Shadi.

Mr. Moepeng was just entering the library as I came down the staircase where the women were cleaning. "*Ke na le nonyane mo offisi!*" (I have a bird in my office!) I said to them.

Instead of the joking response I expected, the three exchanged alarmed glances. Shadi looked at me sternly. "*Ga pay* (repeat yourself)," she said.

I didn't know the word for owl, but I repeated.

I saw from their expressions they understood. Shadi's face became a mask of open-mouthed fear.

"Mr. Moepeng," she called, following with rapid fire Setswana, and then beckoned to the other cleaning woman. The two women set down their wide brooms and ignored me as they headed up the stairs with Moepeng.

I followed, but clearly the three were on a mission separate from mine. They weren't interested in my reactions. He entered the office first, then the women. I joined them and we crowded in the doorway. The large bird spread his wings to their full extent and the women gasped.

The two women conversed rapidly and then left the office.

Mr. Moepeng turned to me, "These birds — 'owls' you call them — go with night, witches and death. If you see them outside, okay, that's where they live. When they come in your place, it is a sign."

He then opened the window as wide as possible in order to give the bird an option for escape. We then corralled the owl into the corner nearest the window and forced it to seek a way out. With difficulty it squeezed through the open louver and took flight.

We stood by the window watching it fly off.

"Very bad luck," Mr. Moepeng said and left the room.

The women returned and told me they would clean the mess off my floor. Their no-nonsense tone of voice meant I was to gather what I needed and get out.

Downstairs, as I was leaving the building, I saw Mr. Moepeng again and he seemed less anxious.

"I don't think our beliefs affect your culture," he told me. "It was just an accident that the bird came inside your office. Probably chased by an eagle."

His tone sounded reassuring enough, but it was clear he wanted to smooth over something that was deeply disturbing. I knew he remained unconvinced by his own words. The women walked past us with a pail and mop, but they wouldn't look at me.

LATER IN THE DAY, as I worked at my desk, Kentse, one of my students, entered the office. I was surprised to see her. She was a quiet woman I hardly knew because in class she seldom spoke. Kentse was accompanied by two other young women I had seen on campus, but did not know at all.

The three found chairs and formed a semi-circle around my desk. Kentse's face was grim. "Mr. Ashford, I have heard a bad report."

I sensed her reluctance to mention the incident. "The owl, you mean?"

She nodded.

"It's nothing to worry about," I said. "Birds are a sign of very good luck in my culture." I noticed that my voice had a chatty, superficial tone.

She fixed me with a gaze that seemed stern and unflinching.

The students were not there to make friendly conversation, but to sit quietly. A voice in my head chattered about all the work I had to do. I wanted to say, I don't have time for this, but there was something peaceful about their company and I said nothing.

After we sat together for fifteen minutes, they stood to leave. Kentse said, "*Sala sentle* (goodbye), Rra."

For the next two days, students entered my office to sit with me. Some of them I knew, several I did not. We sat together quietly until they parted. Their attitude seemed to be that I was a newcomer to their part of the world. There were powers at work here that I wouldn't understand. They were here to help and I finally gave in. I gave up any plans to do my office work.

In the afternoon of the second day of these vigils, a young woman named Obolikile visited. In class she always seemed to take in everything with her large, round eyes. She told me she had heard about the owl. She and I sat quietly and when I was feeling peaceful, she stirred in her chair.

Calmly, she looked around the room, her eyes attentive to every detail, as if surveying the scene of a crime. After several minutes she said in a solemn voice, "You must pay attention to this." She paused. "It is a sign. An owl is a serious thing."

She said no more, but rose from her chair and left.

I thought about the visits of the students to my office, the concern of Mr. Moepeng, Shadi, and the others. This was a village trying to help, but I had not been receptive to them. If anything, I wanted all this attention to go away. But, as I began to tally all of the Africans I worked with who felt genuine concern for me, I began to reevaluate my stance. I had been nonchalant about the incident and I'd told them, "In my culture, birds are good luck."

But what's that about? Are birds really good luck? Who invented that myth? Am I just playing the role of invulnerable White Man?

The Africans had made it clear: this was serious. For the first time, I began to wonder if I shouldn't also take the owl's visit more seriously. Perhaps, I had to acknowledge my lack of understanding and just accept their help. Say it again, *accept their help.*

### III

"I HEAR YOU'RE BATCHING IT NOW," Patrick said, his tone of voice self-consciously informal. "Welcome to the club." Patrick winked to let me know it was a joke. His wife had returned to England to register the boys in a boarding school. I had become a member of the "club" when my wife traveled home to be with her elderly mother.

It was a Friday morning in early September and we were in the staffroom — the same place where the two of us had been introduced only a month and a half earlier.

"You look slim and fit," I told him.

My comment was an attempt at flattery on my part. In his wife's absence Patrick had thrown himself into physical exercise; every afternoon, I saw him playing soccer with students on the sports field. After the soccer match, he rode his bicycle between the college and his house, a distance of 15-kilometers. Some days he pedaled to Francistown, forty kilometers from the college.

"Exercise agrees with me," he said. "I've shed twenty pounds."

I looked up at the taller man, at his gaunt face with every bone sharply delineated, his eye sockets and jaw visible under shrunken skin. I didn't know what I was seeing. *Is Patrick the picture of health? Or is he ill?*

Customarily Patrick wore his usual navy blue blazer and pressed gray slacks, but since his wife had left, he had thrown himself into exercise. There were many times I observed him usually donning a t-shirt and shorts before riding his bicycle to his house.

He told me his wife had extended her stay in England. "The task of enrolling the boys is taking longer than we anticipated." A certain breeziness in his tone made me think I was getting the cover story version of events. His reserve would never allow him to acknowledge emotion or inner conflict, but I could imagine phone calls from England . . . *Patrick, I can't just go off and leave them. They'll be so lonely . . . I feel as if I'm being wrenched.* Then perhaps the sounds of Barbara sobbing over the phone as he listened helplessly until he felt reduced to being a little boy himself.

"She could be gone another six months," Patrick said. "But it's important to help things get settled for the boys." He set his cup down and rocked on his heels, hands folded behind his back. Except for his emaciated, ascetic face, an observer might have mistaken him for a man talking about real estate. "And Gen?" he asked. "When does she return?"

"Ten more days," I said. "We talked on the phone last weekend." Ten days sounded like forever to me, but far better than six months. Six months sounded like a prison sentence.

Patrick reminded me that he and his wife had discussed the pros and cons of their boys going to school in Botswana or in England. It was a story he told over and over. I had heard the rationale repeated a dozen times. In Botswana, the family would be together, but they would not get an adequate education. In England, the boys would get the kind of education the parents had received, but it meant a separation of months between school holidays.

"In the end," he told me, "education means more for the boys' future. They'll go to work someday in a competitive world."

Patrick's energy lifted when he talked about the competitive world. He was a booster. "They need computers! They need to be where they use computers in the schools." He gave me a stiff-upper-lip kind of smile. "Everyone will be stronger for enduring the distance."

His words reminded me of a quote I'd heard somewhere: "What doesn't kill me will make me stronger."

He bent to pick up his cup and I heard the rattle of china as he moved away. "I'm going to sneak off early today. Tennis match at the club."

After we parted, I checked my mailbox. One telephone message and a utility bill. "Patrick Sherwood" was written on both, but his mail kept showing up in my box, which was clearly labeled "John Ashford."

Patrick was gone by that time. *I'd hand him the message and bill on Monday.*

CLASSES WERE CANCELED for a week of mourning, but on Monday morning, a few instructors came to the staff room. I found myself in a group gathered around the man who had been playing tennis with Patrick when he died. I felt some irony realizing that I stood in the same spot talking with Patrick the previous Friday. I caught myself looking around the room. My eyes searched, trying to locate the Englishman in a blue blazer and gray slacks, the tall man with the thin face. I had to keep reminding myself Patrick wouldn't be there anymore.

Dave Stebbing was Patrick's regular tennis partner. Everyone used his last name, no Mister, just Stebbing. A white Rhodesian, his family had been driven out during the civil war, before the country became Zimbabwe, and he received his education in South Africa during the Apartheid era. Africans on the staff usually avoided him, but a few joined the circle to hear what he had to say that morning.

Stebbing had a reputation for a paint-by-the-numbers approach to higher education. Some suspected that he didn't think African students could learn any other way. And any time I listened to him, I copped a skeptical attitude. My feelings towards him had been formed a few months earlier when he first came to the college. Stebbing and his wife worked on a landlord for thirty days to get a Peace Corps Volunteer evicted from an apartment in Francistown so they would have a place to live. Later, he told me, "If housing is scarce, isn't it better to have two people living in a unit, rather than just one?"

That Monday, he faced the group in the staff room as if he were standing before a first-year class. "We left the college about 3:00," he told the circle of people surrounding him, "and drove to the Francistown Club." The Francistown Club was a whites-only private club.

Stebbing held his teacup and saucer in the flat of his palm. With his clean-shaven face, white shirt, and smart tie, he reminded me of a school boy giving a report: How I Spent My Weekend.

"We played about half an hour, when Mr. Sherwood stopped, saying he felt a little bit dizzy. 'Are you okay to keep on playing?' I asked. He said, 'Yes, I haven't had enough to eat. That's all.' We carried on."

There did not seem to be any reason for Stebbing to refer to his friend as, Mr. Sherwood, except there were Africans in his audience. He would not be the one to breach the rules of formality between races.

"About half past five he put his hand to his head." Stebbing paused briefly, as if he remembered an important detail. "Actually, at that point I was heading away to collect some balls, when he collapsed on the ground. I ran over and another man in a nearby court went to make a call. I got to Mr. Sherwood and his eyes were just staring. He was unconscious."

Stebbing looked up, collecting an insight. "So, I imagine," he said thoughtfully, "he went directly from a conscious state to an unconscious state."

Stebbing continued in his manner of storytelling, telling of the death of his friend by describing the friendly and highly competent European doctor, describing the drips and oxygen mask that were attached, and the cardiograph machine that monitored Patrick's heart.

"It was hardly beating at all," Stebbing said.

While he described the wonders of European technology, the heroism of doctors and himself, I filled in the gaps with silent sarcasm, managing to surprise myself with the depth my disdain toward Stebbing.

Stebbing ended with a short summary of final methodologies to save Patrick. "For thirty minutes, they gave injections of adrenaline and electric shocks to try to get his heart started again. But there was no response. So, after the doctor said there was no reason to continue, I returned to college and telephoned Mr. Sherwood's wife in England."

He was finished. Stebbing looked at his watch and, apparently feeling he had done his duty, moved to put his teacup away. The group dispersed and I went to check my mailbox. The only piece of mail was a general notice to teaching staff announcing a meeting later in the week to plan for the dedication of the new college.

Another instructor, an African man, stood near his mailbox and grumbled, "I hope they are not serious about going ahead with this dedication ceremony."

A FEW OF THE TEACHERS met daily in the staffroom during that week of mourning, mostly Africans, occasionally a Dutchman or a teacher from Bangladesh. I first saw the group of men circled around a low table on Tuesday. Initially, I was reluctant to join them, thinking they had private business to discuss. But my Ugandan friend, Joseph, waved me over. After that, I joined the group every morning. Our conversations were random and any rumor was grist for the mill.

Gen was not scheduled to return until the following week and it was fortunate that I found these men. Getting together with them gave me a reason to get going in the morning. I'd begun to feel a confusion of feelings that attacked me physically. My shoulders ached, my arms felt heavy. A headache kept me awake at night. The feelings were at their worst when I woke up in the morning. But each day I dragged myself from bed to join the conversation with the other instructors.

After I entered the circle on Tuesday, I heard one of the men say to the group, "You've heard about the autopsy?"

Another answered, "I heard an autopsy took place. As yet, I've seen nothing concrete."

Others shook their heads. No one had heard.

When the subject turned to the forthcoming opening of the college, several men in the circle expressed the wish that it would be canceled. But on Wednesday the *Botswana Guardian* included a banner headline, "Minister to Open Tonota College." Referring to a visit to our school by the Minister of Education, the article removed any doubt the program would take place as scheduled.

Another article I had barely noticed appeared on page two of the same issue with the caption, "Headmaster Dies Suddenly." The death of the headmaster at one of the village elementary schools was the main topic when I sat down with the group in the staffroom on Thursday morning.

"I had dinner in his compound just last week," a Zambian man said. "I knew Mr. Kololo very well." Mr. Tembo, the man speaking, was a math teacher at the college. His face was a copper shade. The tan color of his safari suit was several shades lighter than his skin. "His death took place on Monday, but the newspaper said nothing about cause. 'Mr. Kololo passed away after a short illness,' was all it said. There was a reference to his 'untimely death.' It sounded for all the world as if it were an ordinary thing."

Mr. Tembo paused and gave the circle a knowing look. "Not exactly," he said. Then he began to relate a chain of events and rumors.

"Everyone knows it was witchcraft," he said. "But no one knows who is responsible. Like many others in his position, Mr. Kololo knew many people. He served on the board of village schools. Professional activities took him all over the country. He earned a good living. There are many people who might be jealous. He may have received an appointment or honor that someone else badly wanted. So there is this possible motive: Revenge. Or perhaps, one of his girlfriends got jealous. Who knows? Revenge or jealousy. This much is certain, Mr. Kololo was not ill. He was an active, healthy man one day. The next day he was dead.

"In the morning, he walked into the cooking area at his school. On a large table he saw the intestines of a goat, recently butchered. He asked the cook what she was preparing, but the cook didn't know what he was talking about. She said she hadn't butchered a goat. Together, they walked back to the table where he had seen the meat. The table was clean."

Mr. Tembo paused and looked around the circle of faces, then he continued. "So, it was sorcery. The work of an n'goma. Within a few hours, Kololo collapsed with pain in his stomach. His friends took him to hospital in Francistown, but nothing could be done."

Mr. Tembo reached for his teacup on the low table at the center of the circle. "The bloody intestines he had seen — they were his own. Of course, at hospital they had an obvious explanation. They said he died of internal bleeding."

The Africans nodded and smiled. A man who had not spoken, said, "Western science has an explanation for everything."

A large man named Mr. Kumalo sat with his arms folded across his chest and nodded in agreement. "It's the same as with Patrick's autopsy," he said. "You've heard by now, I assume. They discovered the cause of death." He emphasized the word discovered in a derisive manner.

Others reacted in a way that meant they had heard something. But I had not.

He continued, "The autopsy used a medical term — pulmonary edema." Mr. Kumalo held out his hands.

Another man spoke up, "I heard that, too. Just what does that mean?"

Mr. Kumalo answered, "As I understand the term, it refers to fluid filling the lungs."

"Isn't that interesting," Mr. Tembo said. "A forty-year-old man, healthy and strong, can collapse. The doctors tell us his lungs were filled with liquid. In other words, he drowned on the tennis court." He smiled sarcastically. "Isn't it a comfort to have the knowledge of Western medical science in these times of grief?"

# IV

AT THE STAFF MEETING on Friday afternoon, I entered the room with my entire body aching. I tried my best to ignore it.

We crammed ourselves into a small classroom where workmen had placed tables in an open U-shape, with chairs placed on both sides of the rows of tables.

The principal was seated at the closed end of the U as the rest of us searched for a place. Seated next to the principal, Mr. Chewe looked half-asleep.

Semi-dazed myself, I slumped into a metal folding chair. I had participated in the week-long observances — the singing of hymns, a memorial program. Now, this crowded room felt like the last place I wanted to be. Besides my aching shoulders and back, a dark cloud of mental despair hung over me that I didn't really understand. How could it be grief? I didn't know Patrick that well. Was it just hearing about death? All I knew was that my emotions were rising to the surface and I was paying a toll in terms of physical pain and mental anguish. I kept reminding myself, Gen will return in four days.

Peter sat a few chairs away from me and when I looked over at him, he looked stressed as well. I hadn't seen him since the day he came into my yard to inform me of Patrick's death. He'd been off campus during the week to attend a curriculum meeting. Peter's face was pale and deeply lined. As bad as I felt, I knew he must have felt worse. Patrick was his friend.

The principal, visibly anxious to get the meeting started, stirred in his chair. In a terse memo to the academic staff he had called this meeting to discuss the dedication ceremony celebrating the college opening on 21 September . . . eight days away.

He rapped his knuckles on the table. "As you know, the first day of the Tonota College school year is to take place shortly. We have some pertinent items to discuss and I'd like to hear your concerns. I want to begin by hearing from anyone who has comments."

Mr. Kumalo usually listened calmly with his arms crossed, rarely saying anything. This afternoon he was the first to speak. "Mr. Principal, I would hope that you might entertain the possibility of postponing or rescheduling the dedication ceremony. No one on staff has given thought to the program. We have all been much too preoccupied."

Another teacher's voice from the other side of the room chimed in, "I agree, Mr. Principal. The event should be postponed. We have all been in mourning. We have lost a week in planning and are still in shock."

Mr. Jeremiah, a Motswana, his hands folded carefully on the desk, spoke in a heavy accent. "Definitely, a delay of some kind is in order." He paused briefly to let his point sink in, then added, "As you may have heard, there has been another unexpected death in the village. Last week, following Patrick's death only by three days, a headmaster at one of the village schools died very suddenly."

At the end of the table, Mr. Tembo, the Zambian I had heard in the staff room and a personal friend of the principal, began to speak. "Two deaths, Mr. Principal," he said. "The headmaster's funeral is scheduled for the same day as the opening. Villagers will be obligated to go to the funeral. It means there will be no village participation. The timing is most unfortunate . . . and unlucky."

Mr. Kumalo spoke again. As a department head, he was a man the principal would be sure to listen to. "The villagers are going to look at this circumstance, two deaths, both men in education, and they will say this is an omen. They are acquainted with the facts of Mr. Sherwood's death and everyone in the village knew Kololo. They won't come to the ceremony, and it cannot be a success without them. As my colleagues have suggested, I think it's important we postpone the date until these events have been forgotten."

A murmur swept through the room and Mr. Jeremiah, who taught religious education, spoke again in a fervent voice, "Sir, the Lord has visited the village and punished us with two deaths."

I looked over at Peter. He hadn't said a word, nor did he appear to want to. Usually these meetings with staff consisted of reports on curriculum issues and he made short speeches in his mellifluous BBC English. His accent was a weapon of power that intimidated everyone in its perfection. Today Peter was silent. Staring at the ceiling, he perched on the edge of his chair like a bird preparing to take flight. I could tell that in this meeting he was uncommitted, prepared to escape at a moment's notice.

The principal had listened and now stated flatly, "There is no chance we will delay the dedication ceremony. Invitations have been sent out and the Minister himself has told me on the phone he will attend. He is the main speaker. I am definitely not going to ask him to reschedule. We will go forward with the planning." Then, he proceeded to sketch out a tentative schedule of tasks. "During the week, the head cook will work with four women to make traditional beer. That is a four- or five-day process and they will have to start early in the week."

Tembo interrupted, "Mr. Principal, there will need to be a sacrifice of beasts."

Jeremiah joined in, "Two very bad omens. Within one week two men have died. This requires the slaughter of a significant number of beasts."

My ears perked up. Slaughter of beasts! The phrase sounded straight from the Old Testament. When I looked over at Peter, his face was now buried in his hands. The discussion of food and beasts seemed to be making him sick to his stomach.

Tembo spoke. "I attended the opening of a junior secondary school recently. Three beasts were slaughtered. This is a college that serves the entire nation. We must slaughter more animals."

I was astounded. *What does this have to do with the college opening?* I wondered. What does the slaughter of animals have to do with the fact two men have died? What does any of this have to do with Patrick?

Jeremiah added, "We have the dedication of a new college and important guests to consider. It would look terribly bad if there was not a sacrifice of six or seven beasts at least."

I had been in hundreds of staff meetings since I started to teach, but I had never heard a discussion about the sacrifice of beasts. I didn't even know what kind of animal they referred to.

But the principal did not seem at all surprised by the discussion. He nodded, "We have donations, in fact. Twelve beasts are available for the event," he said. "Farmers are contributing the animals and I have requested several men to drive out to cattle posts and collect them."

He looked toward the corner of the room. "Twelve beasts have been promised," he repeated. "Can we feed 2,000 people with twelve beasts?" His words were directed to an Irish woman, the head of the home economics department. Her teachers and students would be responsible for food preparation at the event. She sat at a table near several of her faculty.

The Irish woman went into a huddle for a hasty meeting with her department. Within a few minutes there was a stir and she said, "Mr. Principal, if the college slaughters twelve beasts, every person attending will be fed approximately four kilos of beef." She was an energetic woman who spoke forcefully. "Based on my calculations, we should slaughter no more than four animals. Any more would be an utter waste. Besides, I am concerned about the number of pots it will take."

The principal gave her a tolerant smile. "I'll leave it to you to borrow the pots you need from village schools."

After passing out a list of assignments for the event, he closed the discussion. Everyone stood amid a clatter of chairs and as people began to file out, I saw Peter in the crowd, still looking miserable. At the end of these meetings, I was used to seeing him chatting with other department heads, shaking hands, patting backs, "touching bases" as I'd heard him describe it. Today however, he kept his head down and disappeared quickly from the room.

THE SLAUGHTER OF ANIMALS was assigned to Joseph, a Ugandan instructor in the agriculture department. He was a short, muscular man, amazingly strong. In the grazing area at the college, I'd seen him handle a sick cow that was on the ground. In order to get it on its feet, he lifted it, first, by the tail, then, by the horns.

For years of my life, before coming to Africa, I'd been a vegetarian and I've never enjoyed seeing animals suffer. The idea of sacrificing beasts, or cattle, was totally outside my experience. As a way to bring closure for grief or reestablish harmony and balance for a successful college opening, it baffled me. Only in Old Testament Biblical stories had I heard of anything like this. I should have found the idea repulsive, but in some way that I didn't understand, the idea began to intrigue me.

Joseph and I had worked on several projects together. I'd written a USAID grant for his agricultural program, and, at the request of the principal, produced a video of cattle being rounded-up and run into a kraal. Joseph narrated the video every step of the way as the animals were guided into a chute, given inoculations, and tested for disease.

After the meeting, I approached him, asking, "Can I go with you?"

"Sure," he said. "It'll be sometime midweek. I'll let you know."

That Friday after I left the staff meeting, I didn't know what to do about the pain in my body. Yet, the intrigue and excitement of a sacrifice unexpectedly stirred something in me and began to occupy my mind. The idea became an obsession.

Over the weekend, at night my room was bright as day. The moon was full and light streamed through my bedroom window.

I had a dream Saturday night.

■

I knew I had left Africa, though I had no idea where I was.

I was walking with two friends along a sidewalk, and then we turned to enter a narrow alley between tall brick walls. It was a big city alley, a canyon, like nothing I'd seen in Africa. After taking only a step or two in the shadows of the alley, I realized my friends were gone. They had disappeared.

*Why had we turned into this alley? Where were my companions?* I wondered.

At that moment three men approached, though they didn't seem to be together. One walked ten or fifteen steps ahead of the others. The first man, wearing a dark cowboy hat and chaps, walked so close, he brushed my arm and I became aware it wasn't a casual thing, there was something intentional in his approach. At first, I thought the man was panhandling. As he passed, he said something, but I didn't understand. "What?" I said.

He turned and faced me, then jabbed a hard finger into my ribs. "*Corpulus!*"

He repeated "Corpulus" until the word began to echo between the walls of the alley as if he was intoning the words of a chant, but it was a signal to the other men — it was the beginning of a ritual.

I ran and a chase began. But the men were like ranch hands working together, professional, and catching me was their work. They did their work without emotion. It wasn't personal. With twirling lariats, they overtook me, and any evasive move worked to their advantage. I felt like an animal in a pen. I ran and dodged, but the reality was clear, I was already caught. My moves only delayed the final noose. I was aware that in a herd, who knows which one will be sacrificed.

Finally, they threw ropes around me and pulled me to an open square where orange flames leapt from a stack of logs. A large pot hung over the fire. I was led to the fire and while they drew out my life I stirred the pot with a long stiletto, and watched.

Bones were scattered everywhere on the ground. They were my bones and my body parts that were to go into the pot. Still stirring the pot, I heard the chant, "Corpulus . . . atone." As I watched the sacrifice, I realized that I was the one being offered.

■

The dream played through my mind all night, with slight variations — men in cowboy hats became men in orange robes with shaved heads — it repeated over and over until the room was filled with the orange light of dawn and I opened my eyes.

A few days passed and Joseph failed to notify me about his plans for the round-up and sacrifice, but I wasn't surprised. When I'd asked him on Friday if I could join him, despite his inviting smile when he said he'd "let me know," I had the impression that this was an African thing — other Africans were going to help, but a Westerner would have been out of place. There were some aspects of the culture Joseph couldn't share with me.

So it was, I missed the ritual.

TUESDAY, I RENTED a powder blue Volkswagen Golf for the five-hundred-mile round trip to Gaborone to pick-up Gen at the airport. I waited for her in the airport building, a large room that served as lounge, baggage claim, customs, and car rental office. In the distance, I recognized her yellow cotton pants suit as she descended the stairs from the 747 and walked across the tarmac. By that time, she'd been in transit for thirty hours. She entered the warehouse-sized building through the double doors; I opened my arms to give her a hug. She allowed the full weight of her body to fall against me.

"How's your mother?" I asked.

"Seemed much better by the time I left."

Gen was perspiring in the heat and I carried her bag to the small car. We hadn't said much by the time she fell asleep in the passenger seat. She dozed all the way home.

That was the day Joseph rounded up the animals.

ON SATURDAY, DRUMMING echoed between the buildings on the campus.

Guests of honor — mostly men in three-piece suits — surrounded the stage.

Young, bare-breasted women danced on a temporary stage with men who wore rattles on their ankles and traditional loin cloths. It occurred to me that yesterday, all the dancers wore their school uniforms. Today, in their nakedness, they threw themselves with abandon into ritual dancing. During breaks, speakers arose to welcome, extol, or introduce other speakers. The speakers all used pompous language and I became increasingly impatient.

To get away from the speeches, I walked to a road that ran along the north side of the campus. The campus maintenance shed, a large ivory-colored metal building was located there and on the loading dock where the school kitchen received deliveries, vats full of traditional beer were being stirred and served. The area had the sour smell of sorghum mash from the brewing.

To the left of the loading area there was a large outdoor cooking pad the size of two classrooms where six huge cast iron pots were simmering over open coals. The missionary-sized pots reminded me of my dream a week earlier. Several men stirred the pots, others sat or visited. The concrete was littered with scraps of bone, gristle, amputated forelegs, and hooves of butchered cattle; the soil around the pad was soaked with blood.

The stench of cooking flesh was overwhelming and it required a conscious effort to stifle my nausea, but I wanted to satisfy my curiosity. Many of my students were working around the pots and vats. I saw a man in a pumpkin-colored shirt and recognized him. It was James, one of my students. He smiled and invited me to join him with a wave. James had a heavy-lidded expression — the effect of the traditional beer, I guessed. He ladled some beer into a dented aluminum cup, which was passed around a circle of students before James handed it to me. I felt their eyes on me as I sipped the thick brew, sour and heavy, from the communal cup.

I passed the cup on to the next man in the circle, and the others looked at me mischievously, as if they found it amusing to see a white man sipping of a Tswana tradition.

My senses were bombarded with the reek of meat, the noise of drumming, and scenes of pools of blood and gristle; my dream kept reappearing in my mind, and I realized what it all came down to.

It was about the omens that appeared weeks ago. It seemed like ages since I'd seen the owl spread its wings and stare at me with round yellow eyes. It occurred to me that Patrick and I were like the cattle — sacrificial beasts. The pain I'd felt all week in my body had been a mystery to me, but now I understood it as something related to being on the receiving end of a bad omen. The owl's appearance in my office was a potent act of witchcraft, but somehow, I had managed to survive.

For the feast, we needed an animal or two, or twelve. What does it matter, how many or which ones? I stood in the circle where another cup of beer was being passed from hand to hand. When the cup came around again, I took my turn and drank the strange brew.

"Sala sentle, Rra," I said to the group, then walked back to the center of activity where drums pounded and a crowd watched the dancing. I found Gen in the crowd. She was wearing a flowered cotton print dress; one she said was cool in the heat. For a few minutes, we stood swaying and clapping in time with the rhythm, watching the young women and men dancing.

Lunch was being served and we walked through a crowd to get into line. People sat on the ground with their food and as we found our way, I saw Peter and Ellen. Peter, busily chewing, gave me a mock salute with his fork.

Things had come full circle. I carried away a tray with potato salad, maize meal porridge, a dish of goat meat, and a bowl of beef stew. We located a sloping, open piece of red earth and sat down. With my tray perched across my knees, I plunged my spoon into the bowl. Looking at the steaming cube of beef perched on the end of my spoon, I paused a minute, took a deep breath, and inhaled the moist warm fragrance.

# The Dean's Garden

WALKING FROM MY HOUSE to my office on the campus in Botswana, it was a familiar sight to see my neighbor, the dean, straddling a black plastic chair, watering his garden. The chair was from one of the college classrooms, but under his nearly 300-pound girth, it looked like a kiddy chair, the thin chrome legs sinking into the red Kalahari sand. Much too flimsy to support a man his size.

"Hello, John," the dean said. I was always impressed by the theatrical quality of his voice, as if he were on stage playing a Shakespearean role. As I walked by, he turned in his chair, took the pipe out of his mouth, and his brown moon face greeted me with a welcoming smile. He often wore a burgundy-colored sarong and a T-shirt bearing a map of Africa. When he rubbed his chest, his big hands covered the Sahara. He patted his tummy, and the Kalahari Desert disappeared under his fingers.

I complimented him on his flowers. "Ah, the flowers are singing to me today," he boomed.

Smoking his straight-stemmed pipe with one hand and holding the hose with the other, he let the water spill into the sand where a channel had been scraped out. Although the trickle of water seemed to disappear into sandy red soil, puddles were forming around the flower beds several feet from where he sat.

The dean's flowers and tomato plants, arranged in a neat, formal line, suggested an English cottage garden. Everyone's garden in the teachers' housing compound seemed to recall another place. Our gardens were dream environments we carried around in our minds. Maybe the dean's style was from Port Elizabeth, South Africa, where he was from. His flowers were not particularly showy or exotic — marigolds, zinnias, and some I couldn't name — but they were profuse. Some people clipped flowers after they turned brown, but the dean didn't fuss. I'd seen marigolds that grew with one large flower per stalk, but the dean's clustered on a bush — a whole clump of greenery and small flowers balanced precariously on one thin stalk. The blooming flowers in his garden received more water than any other plants in the neighborhood. Yet inevitably, in this desert region all plants turned brown and, in his garden, spots were already forming on the stems.

It was July, the cool season in the Kalahari Desert, and the weather was dry, but for me, a native of Seattle, the days felt like comfortable summer weather.

"Your tomatoes look healthy," I said. "I'm going to come by and steal some when they're ripe."

The dean chuckled. "When my tomatoes are ripe, you are welcome. Come and help yourself."

I waved and wished him a pleasant day.

The dean had come to the college, initially, as a teacher. His teaching style was unorthodox, but very effective.

During the school year, his classes staged Hamlet in the auditorium. Recently he'd cast a young man in the lead for this year's production who also attended my class. I thought it was a curious choice because the man had a great deal of difficulty with the English language. But playing the role of Hamlet during the performance, he was on stage for two hours and had memorized his part perfectly.

Any time I traveled in Botswana, I met people who asked about the dean. Most of them had been students in his classes; they all spoke English beautifully and all of them idolized him. Of course, they knew him before he was the dean and referred to him by his first name, Livingston. People were drawn to him, in part, because his credentials went beyond the usual academic degrees.

In South Africa he'd grown up under Apartheid and became an activist. I was told he knew Nelson Mandela personally. Eventually, the dean and his wife left South Africa to live as exiles in England. I asked about his wife one day and he told me, "She found a great deal of pleasure with her job in England and chose to remain." I interpreted his explanation as a way of saying, she didn't want to return to the racial politics of South Africa.

During the time I knew the dean, my respect for him grew. It was very clear that in the struggle against Apartheid, he along with many others devoted their lives to protest for the right to be treated with dignity, and it was a protest on behalf of everyone, not simply an effort to gain an advantage over someone else. Their struggle was an all or nothing pursuit, everyone gained their rights, or no one did.

Nearly every day, college administrators visited the dean's house to discuss problems. Everyone knew where they could find him and as he listened attentively, water from the hose trickled over his flowers. Passing by, I caught occasional snatches of their conversations, "Well, you see, if the people in the hostels won't enforce the rules . . .." The resonance of his voice reminded everyone that he did not deal in secrets. "Yes, and you know I have talked to that young man many times. I have told him myself . . .." Anything he said might be repeated, but not whispered.

I witnessed more of the dean's style at an assembly after a group of students had returned from their teaching practice, and shortly after I had joined the faculty. As part of the program, the principal intended to introduce new lecturers and a dozen of us took our seats in a long row of molded black chairs at the front of the auditorium. When the time came for the meeting to begin, however, we sat facing a nearly empty hall. There were no more than twenty students in an auditorium built to seat 200.

The principal fumed and paced as a few students trickled in. "Where are they?" he muttered. Finally, out of absolute frustration, he launched into a tirade about a student body that could not muster the energy to attend required events.

The dean, seated in one of the auditorium seats facing the row of new staff, spoke up, "If perhaps we could delay the start just a few more minutes, I am sure the others will arrive."

The principal stopped talking and sat down, obviously trying to control his anger.

At that moment, the dean caught my eye and spoke up. In his voice there was almost a tone of apology, "You see, John, these students have been on their teaching practice in very remote areas." He drew out the word v-e-r-y to allow me time to visualize just how far and how remote. "All over the country there are schools. Our students have been working in places far from the nearest store. They weren't able to get soap or toothpaste." It was clear that his words, though directed to me, were meant for the principal. "I know for a fact that some of these students were simply desperate this morning for basic things. Today, they have returned after seven weeks where they were without the necessities for basic hygiene. They simply had to go into town."

After a brief pause, the principal felt we had to begin. More students had arrived, but there were still only about thirty in the large room.

His emotional tone much calmer, the principal began by saying, "It isn't fair for me to express my frustration with the poor turnout to those of you who have come to the meeting . . .," but then he went on to express his disappointment with the lack of turnout. Finally he proceeded to introduce the new lecturers, and praise the fact that staff at this new college was growing at such a fast rate.

When the meeting broke up, the dean walked away surrounded by an entourage of several younger teachers, one or two students, and a department head. As he repeated his sorrow at the fact these students had been without the necessities for basic human cleanliness, a few of the teachers filing out of the hall exchanged skeptical glances. All of us were aware that the students were on campus visiting with friends in the hostels or watching a video in the dorm. After all, they'd also gone without watching television for six or seven weeks.

But the dean's defense of the students wasn't really about the need for soap and toothpaste. What mattered was to have the principal consider the problems he'd create if he attacked the student body in anger or treated them with disrespect.

Respect seemed to be the value the dean held most dear and showing respect was the same as teaching respect. In the confrontation with Apartheid, respect had been the source of rebellion. Now, for him, it had become a personal sacrament. Respect had been the path to freedom and it was something he would not compromise. Sometimes it meant that he wouldn't admonish a student directly. He much preferred to send out a memo and, in keeping with his ethical standard of openness, the memos in his usual flowery language went out to everyone.

But as I learned, not everyone appreciated the dean's non-confrontational style. During my first meeting with the academic board, critics had their chance to express their displeasure. The late August meeting was called to order at 9:00 a.m. by the deputy principal. Third term was about to begin, and for several days the weather had been cold and windy. The meeting room was frigid. Everyone dressed warmly expecting the meeting to last all morning. Teaching staff, department heads, and administrators in attendance were from all over Africa, a handful from the British Isles, several from India and Bangladesh. I was the only attendee from North America.

Most of the morning's business had to do with a new agricultural program. That was followed by announcements and reports, and the last item listed on the agenda was titled, "Student absenteeism from class."

A department head had put the last item on the agenda because, as she complained, "Students have only to talk to the dean in order to get an excuse to leave campus and miss class." They were being given excuses to leave on flimsy grounds. "Their family called them home . . ., falsely they claim they are sick . . ., they say they are going to visit a sick relative. But, nobody ever confirms the truth of these excuses," she said.

The dean replied, "They talk to me, yes." His hands were folded on the table. "It is my responsibility to issue exit permits."

Another department head said, "A student will wander over to the dean's house and, automatically, he has an excuse. There is no policy."

"There is no need for written policy," the dean answered. "People ignore written policy."

Someone said, "Students must provide evidence of necessity . . . or they should not have permission to leave the college."

The dean, seated in the front of the room next to the deputy principal, began fidgeting in his chair. "When the students come to me," he said. "If they have a valid reason, I will of course issue a permission form."

"But they should not be given excuses to abandon their classes."

It was becoming clear that this discussion was not going to result in a solution.

At 12:30, the deputy, who had been chairing the meeting, announced he had a prior appointment and left the room, making the dean acting chairman. "I have lived in a traditional society in Africa," he said. "I know occasions arise that are vital to the well-being of students and their families. Consider also, some students are helpful to the college. They work hard for us. We must bend the rules on occasion. We have an obligation to listen to them with understanding."

"Don't these students have a responsibility for their academic work?" one of the department heads asked.

The dean said, "It is my nature to feel sympathy for students. I will not and I cannot do work that is not in keeping with my character."

Someone commented, "We're wasting our time."

Pulling on a floppy, blue wool cap, the dean rumbled, "I am looking for a way to adjourn this meeting." There were one or two brief announcements before he rose from his chair and walked out the nearest door.

The next morning I spotted the dean walking around the campus, smartly dressed in a sport coat and tie. The cold wind had abated; the morning was cool but sunny. The air calm.

"Good morning, Livingston," I said.

"Good morning, John. It's a nice morning," he said. "Finally."

HALFWAY INTO THE TERM, the hot season began, making afternoon air feel like the inside of an oven. At the same time, rumors began floating about the dean's impending retirement.

Along with the hot season, the drought, and the rumors, the dean had problems around his house to deal with as well. Snakes began appearing, apparently attracted by the water in his garden. For several days, he worked cutting back plants and getting rid of grass in order to eliminate hiding places for the snakes. One morning, I saw a four-foot-long gray snake emerge from some vines and slither into the dean's yard. Later in the day, when I told him, he was visibly upset.

Soon afterward, the rumors about the dean's departure were confirmed when the new man, hired to take his place, arrived for a tour of the campus and a house was designated for him in the teacher housing compound.

A week later as I headed off to meet my eight o'clock class, the dean's yard was covered with powdery ash. The dean, wearing his sarong and Africa T-shirt, stood in his yard while a woman raked ash and debris. Several bushes had been burned since the previous day.

Two trees were left standing, but the lower branches were singed. The remaining flowers, were scorched and black, their fragile stems looked brittle.

The dean did not look happy. He greeted me in his booming voice, "John, this is the end of my garden. Last night I killed two snakes. I did not know what would happen with this drought. You know snakes have no water in the fields, so they come here, to my garden. Well, you know I cannot have it. I have told you many times before that I would die if any of my visitors were bitten. Today, I am paying this woman to clear my yard. This is the end of my Gethsemane."

Dust swirled around the woman's rake and small tornadoes of ash coiled in the air around the dean's feet.

I told the dean how sorry I was about the snakes in his garden.

He didn't seem to pay attention to my words. "The world has changed, John." There was a lightness in his voice and he sounded optimistic. "This is my last year. I am retiring. It's a good time for me to return home. Things are changing in the South and I'll see if I can make a contribution there."

I'd been feeling a loss knowing about his departure, but clearly it was my personal loss, not the dean's. The dean was adapting, and it was good for me to see that his optimism had returned.

His yard looked terrible and the stirring of ash around the dean's feet meant the destruction of his dream here. But that ash would settle in the sand and enrich the soil. I knew he was moving on to find another role where he could settle in and be comfortable. He was an excellent teacher and I was sure he would find a job consistent with his own personal code. I knew also, that eventually he would encourage his new students to improve their lives, and teach them about respect. I had no doubt of it. And I imagined that somewhere there would be a new garden for him.

He and I waved, a parting wave, then I continued on my way.

# Topo

IN THE LATE AFTERNOON my classes at the college were over for the day, and I took my usual walk up the road that led out of the village and into the African countryside. Thorn trees lined the rutted, dusty track. Scrub brush grew along its edge bearing hard fruit, nature's version of tough love in the Kalahari.

In the distance, I saw dust stirred by a donkey cart, but as the cart approached the village it jerked, lunged, and then stopped. The animals seemed aimless and the cart weaved from one side to another. It stopped and then lurched forward crazily.

I thought the driver must be drunk and giving confusing signals to his donkeys, but as it got nearer I could see the driver wasn't drunk. Sitting high up on a crude wooden seat with a friend beside him, I recognized the driver as a young man named Topo, a former student. Plainly, he had no idea how to direct the donkeys and his lack of skill slowed his progress. But it didn't stop him. Nothing stopped Topo.

I'd gotten to know Topo when I was new to the village — he was one of my students at the secondary school. I had been teaching there for only a few weeks when I attended my first staff meeting, and Topo was the main item on the agenda. Mr. M'nkundla, the headmaster was being taken to task by the teachers for his failure to properly discipline the boy. A dignified man with skin the color of light coffee, the headmaster sat in the circle listening to comments. As usual, he was impeccably dressed, wearing a tan sport jacket, starched white shirt, and dark tie.

"He needs to be beaten soundly," one of the teachers said of Topo.

"Why is this boy even allowed to stay in school?" asked another.

The question suggested the rejection of a child, something that almost never happens in a village in Botswana. When students were sent home, they were expected to return as soon as possible with a parent for a parent-teacher conference. It was a measure of the degree of frustration with Topo that someone would suggest sending him away.

I was seated on a hard wooden chair slightly outside the circle with the other expatriate teachers on the staff. Near me, sat a woman from India. An Australian teacher of English was across the room. There were two men from Zambia, teachers of math and science. All of us had felt our share of annoyance with Topo, but we listened in silence.

I was surprised to hear the headmaster being chided for his leniency. A week after I arrived he had spoken to me sternly for being too soft. He wanted a more authoritarian presence, someone who used the cane to keep students on their best behavior. He was disappointed with this white-skinned, middle-aged man who refused to strike students. I told him, "I quit a perfectly good job to come to teach here. I didn't give up a career in America to beat African children."

Now, the shoe was on the other foot and *he* was being deemed too soft. Across the room, he sat quietly taking in the comments, occasionally jotting a note on a pad, or calling attention to a matter of process. He showed no visible reaction to the scolding tone of the teachers' voices or the direct accusation that he was coddling a student.

TOPO'S GIVEN NAME was a shortened form of a much longer phrase in the Setswana language that meant "this is the child I have requested from God."

In my afternoon class, however, he showed no awareness of his divine origins. He squirmed in his seat for two hours. If he had been in an American school his impulsiveness and acting out would get him a diagnosis of ADHD. His attention span barely carried him five minutes into any assignment. Thinking deeply or concentrating on a classroom task was not his thing. On a typical day he twisted in his chair midway through a short study time to steal an essay book or to copy another student's work. A minute later, I'd see him throw a pen to a friend across the room. After that, he pointed and convulsed in laughter at the antics of a classmate. In those moments of action, his eyes sparkled with the thrill of the moment and the companionship of his friends — or "partners in crime" as I sometimes thought of them.

My reluctance to use corporal punishment on my students did not mean that I didn't feel frustration with his behavior. But even if I'd become more authoritarian, it wouldn't have made any difference. Topo was in constant trouble in all his classes.

Annoying as his behavior was in class, he was always good natured. There was never a time when I saw him display anger. On our once-a-month Cleanup Day when students swept, washed windows, and waxed floors, Topo was a great help. He loved physical activity. He reminded me of young men I'd known in Seattle, whose personalities seemed to change when they played sports, worked, or created something with their hands.

EACH DAY SCHOOL BEGAN with a gathering on the grounds for a ten-minute assembly. The headmaster or the deputy headmaster presided over the singing of a hymn and a Bible reading.

One morning, the deputy made a few announcements after the brief prayer, and then added, "I want to see these students immediately after assembly in my office."

Everybody knew that anyone whose name was on that list had an appointment to be beaten. The deputy ended his list in a humorous tone, ". . . and my good friend, Topo." It was a line that got a laugh from the assembled student body.

Others laughed, but it made my heart sink to see him that morning. Even Topo, enjoying the attention, joined in the laughter. But then he stood still for a moment as if frozen to the spot. Silhouetted in the sunlight, I saw his large head and broad shoulders that tapered down to narrow hips. Pausing in the middle of the school grounds, he looked around as if expecting help. As I watched, it made me wonder what he was thinking.

When he finally moved away from the assembly towards the administration offices, he wasn't performing for his friends; nothing about his actions seemed comical. His rhythmic, rocking, shuffling walk — usually Topo's form of "cool" — instead, seemed more like a form of controlled turmoil. His small, almost delicate, arms and hands were pressed tightly to his sides as if bound by a rope. I had the impression of a large person, almost adult, whose torso had withered. His head and shoulders, too large for the rest his small body, moved back and forth with the rhythm of his gait. His feet placed one ahead of the other, his bulk tapering to that single point making contact with the earth.

TOPO'S BEHAVIOR HAD BECOME an agenda item at the staff meeting this time because he'd crossed a line and the headmaster began the discussion by outlining the facts for the teachers. Apparently, the police had come to school to talk to Topo about a theft in the village. His misbehavior had been elevated to criminal activity.

Topo had been living by himself in a mud-walled thatched hut. His mother disappeared and a neighbor woman, realizing he wasn't getting enough to eat, invited him to stay in her compound. She fed him for about a week, but one day when she returned from doing errands she found that money was missing — twenty pula — from a bag stashed under her mattress. The woman was furious that this boy she had fed would steal from her. She called the village police. The headmaster added that the woman continued to feed Topo, but she no longer would let him enter her house.

After hearing the story, a teacher at the far end of the room spoke, "This one — Topo — he is in the office of the deputy one day. He is in the office of the headmaster the next day. This goes on week after week. If it were anyone else, he would have been sent from school after three visits. Why is this boy getting such favorable treatment?"

A buzz of conversation began around the room and without waiting for the headmaster to recognize her, another teacher shouted angrily, "How many strokes is he getting when we send him to you?"

The teacher had spoken out of turn and the headmaster reminded everyone in the room that all comments must be directed to the chair, meaning himself.

Despite his best efforts, however, the discussion became noisy. Members of the staff argued that it would be more effective for teachers to beat the students as soon as the offense occurred. When a student is sent to the deputy or the headmaster, the student is not seen immediately and may not receive the beating for two or three days, they said.

I looked around to the other expat teachers. They seemed as puzzled as I was by the arguments. The young man was already receiving beatings from the headmaster and the deputy several times a week, and it puzzled all of us why more would be better. None of the punishments seemed to change Topo's behavior.

The headmaster restored order by reminding teachers there is a prescribed manner for administering punishment. One can only use a stick of a certain size, girls cannot be struck on the buttocks, and no one may be hit on the head. He stressed that it is important to follow the rules and have a witness. Even if students do not receive punishment immediately, it is better to refer those matters to the administration in case of a complaint by the student or by parents.

In the case of Topo, he went on, "He is not receiving special treatment. As a student here, he is a member of our family, and as any one of us would with a troubled member of our own family, I have talked with him, counseled him, and I have administered beatings to him. But with this one, this boy, Topo, I cannot close my eyes to the damage that he has suffered. He is emotionally scarred. He is a problem here at the school, but will that problem go away if we turn him loose on the village? I do not think so. I think he will be in jail. And then what have we accomplished? Here is a boy — a child really — whose mother has beaten him mercilessly and deserted him. Can you imagine? She tried to kill him. She tied him to a tree. Beat him on the head. Look at the scars on his head sometime."

The headmaster turned to set his notepad on a table, and then continued, "I admit that I have a soft spot for Topo when I realize the cruelty he has endured. I think he deserves a chance to succeed at something. I think he deserves to belong somewhere. In good conscience, I cannot turn this boy out of the school as long as I think there is a chance for him here."

Everyone had apparently had their say and even the headmaster seemed to tire of the matter. By the time he ended the discussion he sounded short of patience. "This administration and this headmaster can be soft. We can be soft when it comes to students who need a second chance, and we can be soft when it comes to teachers who sometimes break the rules. I can be understanding when I see the circumstances. I do not report everything. However, do not think that if you ask me to be unbending and hard to the extreme with students that I cannot be hard, as well, when it comes to asking wayward teachers to toe the line."

IN LATE JUNE, I TRANSFERRED to the college and for many months saw nothing of Topo, until that afternoon when I walked up the road leading away from the village. The ruts were deep and the sand was mixed with the dung of the usual travelers there —

cattle, goats, and sheep. Occasionally I saw a donkey-drawn wagon hauling water, but I'd never seen a wagon out of control until I saw Topo, sitting atop a crude wooden bench above the animals he was supposedly driving.

The well-dressed teenage boy next to him was doubled over with laughter. The cart weaved back and forth, but though Topo seemed aware of the humor in the situation, he tried desperately to concentrate on his task. For my part, it was humorous to watch, but I was also happy to see that Topo had a friend.

In his left hand he held the reins and in his right, the whip, but Topo was clueless as to how to use either. Some drivers flicked the whip over the backs of the animals, not touching them, just letting it crack in the air above to remind the donkeys who was in control. But, these donkeys had the upper hand and there was no doubt as to who was in control.

When they slowed, Topo holding his whip, yelled at them. Then he whistled. Finally, after getting no response from the donkeys, he bent over in laughter. The two young men acted like the giggling schoolboys they were.

When the cart came close enough, I greeted him, "Dumela, Topo."

He recognized me and struck a momentary pose — Topo, donkey cart driver. For a brief, formal instant that deceived no one, he played the part of a student observing decorum in the presence of a teacher.

". . . 'Mela, Teacher," he answered.

His sudden formality was unexpected and I smiled.

*Tsamaya sentle* (Travel well), Topo, I started to say. But at that moment, the donkeys decided to bolt off at full speed while the whip hung limp in the driver's right hand. As the cart tore off, I could hear the laughter of the two young men.

I stood watching the cart disappear in a cloud of dust and realized I was still smiling. The village had continued to take him in. He'd been nourished, embraced, and befriended. The village was his hope. Also, I saw that like myself, Topo was not a born whip wielder.

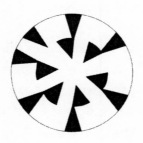

# Boycott

NOVEMBER, 1991. It's almost a year to the day that my wife Gen and I came to Botswana with the Peace Corps and we've been in this village for ten months, each of us assigned to schools here.

It should be spring in the southern hemisphere, but the hot season has come on strong and the steady east wind carries a curtain of dust that surrounds the village, seeps into the house, and makes the weather seem oppressive. The fine dust in the air has Gen coughing and her cough has kept us both awake for several nights. This morning there is a measure of relief with a cooling fog that hangs over the fields outside my window.

A few minutes ago she left, riding her bicycle to the secondary school, but I'm still sitting in the house sipping my morning tea and feeling lethargic. It's a morning when I don't want to do anything productive.

Out in the fields goats are bending the mopane trees to get at the new green leaves near the top of the brown, dry branches. One goat bends the tree and two or three others join the devastation. The trees already look dead and the goats are stripping them even further, but a few clumps of green are still visible. The mist this morning brings some moisture, and moisture is the only hope in this arid world of brown twigs.

Though there are no regular classes this week at the teachers' college, I don't have the luxury of staying home. I've scheduled a tutorial session this morning with my classes to help them prepare for their exams next week, and so at a quarter to eight, I head out my door and start down the paved road that circles teacher housing.

Even through my shoes, the coarse sand feels cool on my feet. It crunches as I walk toward our gate. I notice weeds have taken advantage of the overnight moisture and opportunistic patches of green appear in the sandy earth.

From a yard across the street I can hear the scritch-scritch-scritch of a broom; a woman is sweeping the gritty red soil. She is bent low and hidden from me behind a hedge. However, in my mind's eye I can see her holding the Tswana broom in her right hand, her left arm folded behind her back. Down the street, several women in other yards are performing the same ritual. It's an act taking place in yards all over Botswana — the ground being swept clean to eliminate hiding places for snakes.

Outside the gate, I turn down a walkway leading to the campus. Vines form a serpentine tangle along both sides and a sudden clattering of dry leaves startles me. I've seen snakes in that vine and I'm watchful as I walk past. But this morning I catch a flash of iridescent blue as two agama lizards chase each other through the leaves.

I don't have to go too far before I spot some uniformed employees, the "industrial class workers," as they are called, who sweep walkways and carry mop buckets into classrooms. The women wear blue dresses with the letters B.G.P. over the breast pocket. Men, tending the grounds, wear brown coveralls with B.G.P. in orange lettering on the back. B.G.P. means Botswana Government Property. But if you ask one of the men about the meaning, he might smile and say, "B.G.P.? It means *Banna Gabana Peletshe* (The people have no food.)" It's a joke going around among the employees.

Last week the industrial class workers were on strike. Their union was pressing the government to raise the monthly salary from 230 pula — about $80 US—to 600 pula. The government's position was that at P230 the employees were earning about P60 too much. Because the positions of the workers and the government were so far apart, I expected a prolonged strike. Sure enough, only a handful of the employees showed up on Monday, the rest of the 75 workers went on strike, but I didn't see any demonstrations or pickets during the week and the following Monday all the striking employees returned to work. By Tuesday afternoon, everyone who had participated was fired. Then, on Wednesday, the jobs were opened for applications and that same afternoon every employee was rehired at a lower starting salary.

My office is in the library and as I approach the entrance, a cleaning lady named Shadi is sweeping near the door. She's one of the workers who did not strike. Her reason was that she is pregnant. Her condition is becoming quite visible.

One day after I became aware that she was with child, I saw her sitting outside eating her lunch and I said to her in English, "You are eating for two."

"Eating for two?" She had a puzzled look on her face. "What do you mean?"

I translated the idea into Setswana — as well as I could — and when she got the meaning she howled with laughter. Eventually, she taught me the correct way of saying it in Setswana, "*O ja dijo ga bedi* (Are you eating for two)?"

The phrase became a joke among the staff and for days people went around asking "Shadi, are you eating for two?" If I was anywhere near, she would look at me, laugh, and say, "Yes, I am eating for two."

My watch says it's nearly eight and I rush to the office to get my study material, then head to the classroom, but when I arrive the classroom is in total disarray. A study group used it and left a clutter of tables and chairs overnight. Doors and windows were left open and the floors and table tops are littered with red dust blown by the wind. Several moths had died — their wings the size of linoleum tiles, twelve inches from tip to tip.

Before I can arrange my notes on the table, I have to sweep aside an accumulation of also-dead gnats.

A movement across the room startles me.

I hadn't seen the cleaning woman hidden behind a table stacked with chairs. She shuffles her broom, gathering a pile of dust and insects and after we exchange greetings, she continues sweeping and dusting while a large black rhino beetle crawls across the center of the room over the dead body of a huge brown spotted moth.

No students have arrived yet and I write several announcements on the chalkboard, then turn to my notes. After a minute the cleaning woman asks, "Are you using the classroom?"

I shrug and answer, "Yes, I am if my class shows up."

She laughs, and I look at my watch. Ten past eight. Paging through my notebook, I try to remind myself of the topics needing to be covered and, at the same time, wonder whether any students are coming this morning. The tutorial is optional, but yesterday a dozen showed up.

At twenty past eight, it's obvious no one is coming and I begin to gather my papers just as a young man enters from a side door. Bright morning sunlight reflecting off a building behind him allows me to see his silhouette, but not his face, but I know he's not one of my students. I ignore him for a second assuming that he's using the classroom as a shortcut, or possibly, is coming to retrieve something he left here. However, he walks directly to the front of the room and stands by the table where I am stacking my books to carry back to the office.

"Good morning," he says, his tone more businesslike than friendly.

"How are you this morning?"

He stands close and it's obvious he's come to see me. "I am not very happy this morning," he tells me. "I am not feeling well at all."

With the bright light behind him I still cannot see the details of his face. He is my height, about six feet, and looks me in the eye.

"And are you ill, then?"

"No, I am not sick. I am very angry."

I'd never seen this young man before this morning, so the exchange puzzles me and I begin to sense that there might be a connection between this fellow's appearance and the fact that my students are not in the room. "Yes, I am quite angry," the young man says. "Your country is about to attack Libya."

I feel a sudden jolt. "Are you sure about that? I hadn't heard about an attack." This is the moment when I realize that I'm being boycotted today. Scouring my brain, I do recall a BBC news report I heard on our radio about Libya the previous evening. But the facts are hazy. I think it has to do with a plane that had crashed in Lockerbie, Scotland. I remember only scattered details. *Sabotage. Suspicions. Involvement of Libyan officials.*

"It's true. Your country is accusing Libya of shooting down a plane."

"Yes, I do remember the incident you're referring to. A plane blew up over Scotland . . . two years ago . . . a bomb in a suitcase, as I remember."

"And now your country is going to attack Libya in revenge."

The young man's tone of voice tells me he's probably nervous. Also, his facts are off the mark.

I'm reminded of my own politics of confrontation in the '60s when I took part in what were called "consciousness raising dialogs" during the Civil Rights Movement. Along with some of my other white liberal friends, I went to a tavern once a week to participate. We sat and listened while black activists berated us. Confrontation was the mode of communication, and those of us with white skin were on the receiving end.

This man's angry tone makes me feel a sense of déjà vu. But he is standing too close and it makes me feel uncomfortable.

In the confrontations of the '60s, the logic seemed to be that because of my skin color I had a share in the responsibility for the misbehavior of previous generations. Not that I begrudged them the accusations, I agreed with them. Also, I had a lot to learn about listening to another person's point of view. In retrospect, all of us benefitted in those situations. The same logic is driving this man. I am the American lecturer at the teachers' college; therefore, I share the blame for American foreign policy.

All the time I'm listening, I try to dredge up more details of last night's news report. He'd said something about revenge. "I didn't hear anything about revenge," I say. "What I heard was that Britain is requesting that the two men responsible be sent there for trial. The news report did not say that an attack was threatened."

The young man's dark eyes are unflinching. He won't let me off the hook until I'm even more uncomfortable than I already am. As my eyes are starting to adjust to the light in the room, I can tell he's wearing a military green T-shirt with a design that I can't quite make out.

"In the dorms, I heard it," he says. "America is about to attack Libya the way they attacked Iraq. America has the military power and they are about to cause more bloodshed."

His words begin to sound like a speech. Slogans flow quickly from his lips, "Watering democracy with blood . . . the blood of people from the third world."

I can't argue with him. Nothing I say will change the way he feels, but I say just enough to let him know I'm listening. When I think he is about finished, I say, "I don't think Libya is being attacked, but I will listen to the news."

"And so will I!" He's turned up the volume — shouting now, as if it's a threat. Then he turns to leave through the door he came in, saying, "I will listen with interest."

I grab my things and go out the other door. While climbing the stairs to my second floor office, I notice a sharp twinge in my lower back, a sign that our confrontation has caused some stress. During the day, the back pain becomes a full scale muscle spasm and I can't sit at my desk. Instead, I invent errands and make up excuses to walk around the campus.

IN THE AFTERNOON, we have our usual power outage and I have the entire library to myself. The desk and catalog are near the entrance, the stacks at the far end. Tables and chairs occupy the center of the room. Working on preparation for my classes, I'm wandering between the card catalog and the library stacks when, out of the corner of my eye, I see a man enter the far end of the library. Through the glare of the main door, he walks across the polished floor, which dazzles with bright reflections. Since it's still uncomfortable for me to sit in a chair, I rest my elbow on a bookshelf and page through a book. I am standing near the back of the large library room where there is light from a window. The man walks toward me and I begin to recognize his silhouette — he's the same man who confronted me this morning. My first thought is there's been some kind of an international showdown and I'm about to be scapegoated.

The fellow wears the same olive green T-shirt and I still can't make out the design. Absurdly, I find myself studying the T-shirt to find some meaning for this second visit. Does it say, "Vive Saddam Hussein?" Maybe I'm looking for some proof of militancy that would allow me to apply the appropriate stereotype.

My mind is on alert, but my body is strangely relaxed as I prepare myself for the coming confrontation. Doing my best to conceal my state of wariness, I say, "Hello,"

Standing a few steps away, he responds, "Hello."

Neutral enough. His tone, not challenging. I wait for the angry remark as he clears his throat. Then he asks, "Do you have a book by Michael Swan?"

Quickly, I switch into acting as a professional librarian and say, "Let's look in the card catalog."

As we cross the library together I can't believe this is a simple reference request. Michael Swan — though I'm not familiar with the name — must write books about radical Middle East politics, or that glorify careers of people like Ghadafi or Saddam Hussein. I find myself anticipating criticism if the library doesn't have his book. So I do my best to sound offhand and prepare him for the possibility we won't find anything. "This is a new library," I tell him. "There's a lot we don't have." My voice sounds as if it's racing a mile a minute. "The collection, as you know, is primarily for teacher training."

At the catalog, I begin shuffling through cards in the drawer, and, to my surprise, I find an entry for Michael Swan — I had thought it might be Swann, but I was mistaken. "Here! We do have something," My rush of relief feels exaggerated. "It's called *Practical English Usage*."

Altogether, we find three titles in the catalog by Michael Swan and then we walk — I practically skip — over to the shelves to find them.

The young man, too, seems elated. "This man, Michael Swan," he says, "writes so beautifully about the English language . . . Aiyy!" He punctuates his statement with a high-pitched yip. "I have only recently done my internship. I taught English in a junior secondary school. It's so exciting to read what Michael Swan has to say about teaching English. His books are stimulating for a person like me, learning to be a teacher."

Almost immediately, the young man introduces himself as David. As we talk, he exudes enthusiasm. He rhapsodizes about his subject and I can tell he's a serious student. Our conversation ranges and he tells me about writers that excite him. Pasternak, Solzhenitsyn, Edgar Allan Poe. He names a few African writers. "You have such a good writer in the United States. His name is Ludlum. Robert Ludlum . . . Aiyy! He is such a good storyteller."

IN THE FOLLOWING DAYS, David regularly stops in at my office to talk some more. On one of those visits, he enters in a state of anger. After he sits down, he tells me he's read something that shocked him. There are animals cooked in America without first being butchered. "Lobsters, I think they are called. I've never seen one, but I read that they are dropped alive in boiling water." David is in disbelief. "It's so cruel!"

I feel implicated. He needs some kind of explanation, but I don't know how to explain it, other than to say, "They have a simple nervous system, I've read."

My answer is not satisfactory. David still wears a quizzical expression.

"I don't eat lobster," I say and he relaxes immediately.

Each time he visits my office, he is wearing his usual jeans and the same green T-shirt he wore the first day I met him. I see now that it has a faded design of Mickey Mouse on the front. That first day, I suspected David had political motives, but now I have a deeper suspicion.

I suspect that my new friend David wants to practice speaking English with me.

# Thanksgiving in the Kalahari Desert

ONE EVENING LATE IN JUNE, Gen and I and two other Peace Corps Volunteers — Marjorie and Ann — had gotten together for dinner, and one of us — I don't recall who — voiced a need to celebrate an American holiday. The rest of us really liked the idea.

"What about Thanksgiving?" someone suggested.

Living in eastern Botswana, all of us knew from soggy, sweaty experience, that November would be outrageously hot with average daytime temperatures hovering around 120 on the Fahrenheit scale. We decided to celebrate Thanksgiving in July.

In the Southern Hemisphere, July was the cool season. Midday, the temperatures were around 75 or 80. Somewhere in the back of all of our minds were memories of dry corn stalks, cool air, abundant food, and cozy gatherings with family. But even in July, we knew we'd be hard-pressed to conjure up the same kind of harvest festival we'd experienced in temperate North America.

Trying to evoke the proper spirit of an American holiday would be a reach. For nearly two years we had focused on establishing rapport with the values of our local African village, studying the culture and language, and functioning in a rural setting on the edge of the Kalahari Desert. People in the village and expats from other countries knew where we came from, but most days, being called an American was just another tribal designation.

Ann, a lovely, dark-haired woman, thirty years of age, was the only member of our group who wasn't a teacher. She volunteered to host the party. Within our group, she had the nicest house and loved to entertain. I was a little vague about her pre-Peace Corps background — she'd been a bank executive of some kind — but I'd felt the power of her personal magnetism. Ann's dark eyebrows and pouty expression left me feeling unsure of myself at times, and I knew I was not the only man who felt that way. In the States I was sure her persuasive powers helped her achieve success.

Ann hinted that she joined the Peace Corps as an antidote for career burn-out, but a broken romance probably had something to do with it. In Africa, her job involved consulting with small businesses and startups. In our village, she managed a small organization that taught trades of all kinds and business skills. At the same time, she seemed to be doing a lot of exploration.

A South African man named George was her current beau. In the spring, George had taken her on a Club Med vacation to an island in the Indian Ocean, but before she left, Ann stopped by for a quick visit with Gen and me. Over a cup of tea in our living room she laughed and said, "I don't know if I'm in love with George, but I'm certainly in lust."

We settled on a day for our Thanksgiving get-together, Ann gave us a beautiful smile and said, "I think George can pick up some of the ingredients." As soon as she said it, I knew he didn't stand a chance. "Possibly turkey and wine from South Africa. Oh, and maybe cranberry sauce?" She knew George would do anything for her.

He was a handsome man with blond hair and eyes an impossible color of blue. He had traveled to the U.S. for military training once and often talked about his fondness for America. Things were bad in

South Africa at the time and I was willing to bet that George wanted out. If I was right, he hoped Ann was his ticket to the U.S. All he needed to do was convince her to marry him.

OUR MENU PLANNED, the rest of us had the problem of arranging transportation to Ann's and since Volunteers were not allowed to own personal vehicles, we decided to invite Jim, a tall, white-bearded Englishman who lived in the area and had a small truck, a *bakkie*. He agreed to pick us up on the designated evening, "around five," which was his way of saying "on the dot."

The African lack of punctuality drove Jim crazy and he always gave a short lecture whenever the subject of time came up. The lecture was delivered as if he was speaking to a mythical audience of Africans, "If you're not going to be there on time, don't say you will be. Why do you say you'll be there at eight when you know darn good and well you have no intention of showing up until 9:30?" His voice raised an octave as he delivered the punch line.

Sure enough, that Saturday night in July, 1992, Jim and his bakkie were outside our door at 4:59. Gen and I were ready. But when we got in the car we had to listen to his lecture anyway.

We had felt a bit of tension asking him for a ride to this party because Jim had been rejected by Ann when she took up with George. We rode over to Ann's house, four people in the cab of his little Toyota, and Jim grew noticeably more moody as we approached the house.

When we pulled up by Ann's small garden of cactus, eggplant, and a few vines of okra, a fiery red 1969 Pontiac — low slung with white leather seats and a decal of the State of Texas in the back window — was parked in front of the house. George's trophy car. He loved all things American. Just the day before, he had flown over the village waving the wings of his light plane. Everyone in the village saw it because there weren't many planes in the area. The Pontiac had been parked at the airport since he first started dating Ann and he drove straight to her house after landing.

THAT EVENING THERE WERE a half a dozen people sitting or standing in the small living room of Ann's concrete block house. The living room and kitchen formed an L-shape, and as George leaned in the archway leading to the kitchen, he held a glass of wine in his hand and seemed to be enjoying himself thoroughly.

Opening a can of beer, I made myself comfortable in a soft chair near a table of snacks. I looked over at George and thought, *why shouldn't he enjoy himself? He played a big part in making it happen.*

On this occasion, he acted every bit the man-of-the-house, though he was actually living a hundred and fifty miles southeast, across the border in South Africa. He worked as a water engineer and presently, was doing a project in Soweto, just outside Johannesburg. But the prospect of a holiday weekend at Ann's place obviously had him feeling his oats.

Along with many other Americans, Gen and I, had boycotted South African products as a protest against Apartheid before we arrived in Africa. It was ironic that the boycott seemed to lose meaning in Botswana, because everything came from South Africa. Besides, changes were afoot south of the border and, although news reports were full of talk of civil war, it was clear the regime was adapting. But that evening, as far as I was concerned, the boycott was at least suspended.

Marjorie, the other Volunteer in our celebration-planning group, taught art in a nearby village. She took a seat on a ledge built into one side of the living room wall. The wall behind her had been painted with a hunting scene copied from a Bushman rock painting in the Kalahari. Above her was a silhouette of an African antelope wounded by a spear. A Bushman hunter stood near her shoulder, bow and arrow uplifted, penis erect. She didn't enter into the general conversation, instead, she sat quietly, sketching. That was her usual way of socializing. Marjorie never flirted or chatted; she preferred to sit alone and sketch. A goblet of red wine sat on the seat next to her and, occasionally, she took a tiny sip insuring that the glass would last her for the entire evening. As soon as she sat down, a cat wandered into the room and jumped up into the seat next to her.

Jim had taken a seat on a couch in the far corner and immediately seemed to enter a silent stupor. I knew he couldn't have gotten drunk that quickly. But staring at the wall, he nursed a can of beer and refused to talk to anyone. Everyone at the party was aware that Jim held a grudge, considering George his rival.

Ann always treated Jim with extreme kindness. She walked over, greeted him, and offered to bring him a plate of finger food. He shook his head and maintained his silence.

Before Ann's arrival in Botswana, Jim had courted Marjorie. Sitting on her ledge seat, she was half turned, the back of her shoulder towards Jim. Gen joined Marjorie on the ledge and the two carried on a whispered conversation under the Kalahari mural.

To the annoyance of everyone, Jim suddenly came to life and called Ann's dog over to him. The dog, a brindle mutt that slept in the grass under a shade tree most afternoons, had been laying curled up near the screen door in the kitchen. She was lovable, but infested with ticks.

The guests were annoyed because the dog kept passing by the low coffee table where snacks and wine glasses had been placed. Ann had already shooed the dog out of the room once, and George even tried to lock her out, until he found it was impossible to lock the screens in the small house. By the time Ann noticed, Jim was stroking the dog's chest and scratching its ears. The dog's wagging tail was dangerously close to toppling glasses or brushing the food.

"The dog is dirty, Jim," Ann said. "I don't want her to get into the food."

Jim rolled his eyes up under his lids, which he clearly intended as a lecherous expression. "She is enjoying having me stroke her chest. Since I enjoy it as well, it's a mutually satisfactory arrangement. She can stay right where she is." Jim looked pathetic.

Ann gave him a look of pity and returned to watching over the preparation of the dinner.

There was a knock on the door frame, and a young man, tall and thin with a shaved head, entered. He stood in the kitchen and smiled as Ann introduced him. "Everybody! This is Frank. He teaches carpentry."

As Frank was being introduced, George shifted abruptly and stared at the newcomer in a way that made it apparent how insecure his position was with Ann.

Frank took a can of Castle Rock beer from Ann's refrigerator and opened it as he took a seat next to me.

"Where are you from?" I asked.

"I grew up in East Germany." Frank tilted his can of beer and sipped. "Now, of course, we're all the same in Germany. My country doesn't exist anymore. Good riddance." He smiled.

Frank spoke American-English without any detectable German accent. "Where did you pick up your English?" I asked.

"My degree is American Studies. Also, I've traveled. Guess that explains it."

Jim opened his eyes and glared at Frank.

Frank continued, "When I finished at the university, I could hardly wait to go to the British Isles. I wanted to hear English spoken in its purest form. On a trip there, I wound up in the west, near Wales. One winter evening I was hitchhiking, and a car stopped to give me a ride. We drove for several minutes in silence, then the driver said, 'Wmff?'"

Frank pronounced the word as something like a bark, a growl, and a question.

Frank continued, "I asked the man, 'Can you repeat?' So the man replied, "'Wmff?'"

Frank took another sip of his beer. "I thought about it, and said to him, 'I didn't understand. Could you please repeat the point you are trying to make?'"

"'Is it warm enough?' the man said, pointing to the heat controls and indicating that he could adjust the heat in the car."

Frank laughed. "I found out people in Wales don't speak English."

We shared stories about travel in the Kalahari. Frank had been to many of the same places where Gen and I had camped. Sipping his beer steadily, as if he was trying to catch up with the rest of us, he became serious. "Before I got this job, I worked in southern Botswana," he said. "I saw things there that surprised me. For instance, a large military installation. Instead of programs for training and employment. I saw a military air base funded by Americans," he said. "It serves some strategic purpose in southern Africa. But it's Cold War politics."

As we talked, Frank had been smiling and laughing, but with this revelation he began lecturing me on the American role in maintaining the military occupation in Europe, the 1990 Gulf War, and military force in American foreign policy. His expression had also changed and he fixed me with a hard gaze, as if he held me directly responsible for American policy. "Then there's all this garbage about the new world order. As if getting rid of Saddam Hussein or defeating Iraq is going to change the world."

I became thirsty all of a sudden and moved to get another beer. "Can I get you more?" I asked.

"I'm all right. Thanks," Frank said.

Jim's eyes had closed again and he sat in silence. Then the dog wandered off and curled itself into a ball near the door, and Jim suddenly roused himself and called the dog back.

"Jim, no," Ann said. "She's full of ticks."

Jim persisted. "Look at the unequal treatment between the dog and the cats in this house," he said.

I couldn't tell if he was joking or simply off the deep end.

"Cats are held on laps or get up into a chair. No one complains. While cats are curled up comfortably, what about this poor dog? All it gets is rejection. It's not fair, and I, for one, will not tolerate the injustice." Jim's voice had taken on an exaggerated tone of protest. "One person in the room, at least, stands for fair treatment for dogs."

"Mad dogs and Englishmen . . . stick together," said a voice from somewhere in the room. I didn't hear who made the remark.

GEORGE HAD RECOVERED from the shock of meeting a potential rival and was moving around the room acting the part of gregarious host. The aroma of poultry roasting in the oven was beginning to make me hungry. I finished my beer and poured myself a glass of wine.

Making conversation, I asked George about his job engineering the pipeline in Soweto.

"A headache," he said. "It starts here and goes like this," his hand drew a picture in the air showing a fall from the top of a hill, straight down a steep bank. "Then it goes right back up." Drawing in the air again, he showed the sharp rise of the water line up the other side. "We're having the damnedest time. It has to be tested for leaks and pressure. We got the leaks plugged, but have real problems with pressure." George shifted from one foot to another. "I don't know what we'll do. The whole thing is poorly designed. I came in on the middle of the job."

George swirled his wine around in his goblet. "My office for this job is in the middle of Soweto. One week on the job and I've seen two beatings. Gangs. Tribal, you know."

His manner and tone of voice suggested that it was general knowledge that all of the incidents we were reading about were tribal, and what foreign newspapers labeled as racial attacks, were really tribal.

"I drive into Soweto and the guard greets me. When I walk around the neighborhood, it's just like the village here — there's no antagonism. I'm the only white in the area and no one's unfriendly to me. In fact, people come to warn me if there is going to be trouble. They show me the best way to drive out to avoid a problem."

George went on to tell me about a Zulu employee who had been chased by a gang on his way to the office.

"He ran into the office and hid down behind a desk. But, you know, that's all tribal. There was no police or white collusion. When I read in the news or hear that the secret police or armed forces are involved in these incidents, I just cannot believe it. If I believed the government was in any way involved there would be no choice. I'd just have to pack my bags and leave. There is just no future in South Africa if that's the case."

George and I had always avoided the subject of South African politics in our conversations. Both of us knew it would only create disagreement. But he had opened the subject, so I said, "A lot of people do believe that police or covert army units are involved. In *The Weekly Mail* I read about examples of government involvement all the time. The papers make a good case."

George nodded, not in agreement, but acknowledging some people believe in government involvement and he repeated, "If I believed that I'd have to pack my bags. If it's true, I see no future in South Africa. No, the problem is tribal. Xhosa against Zulu. No one has ever proved the government is involved."

"But the government has pitted one tribal group against the other. Since the 1940s it's been government policy to encourage and capitalize on tribal rivalries."

He nodded again, "Well, that's been part of British colonial strategy for ages, hasn't it. Divide and conquer. Rule by dividing the opposition. East Africa, Kenya, India. The British have done that all over the world."

"But the British haven't ruled South Africa for eighty years." I felt on shaky ground talking about South African history. "Look, I can believe it's tribal warfare. But, it's encouraged by the government. Maybe the rivalries began like gang fighting, but they've graduated to automatic weapons. That raises the stakes." Every week, newspapers *had* carried stories of massacres and bloodshed.

I skirted some of the issues. There were things I knew, for instance, that I did not want to mention. George was a former officer in the

173

South African Defense Force and I'd heard him reminisce about old times. Leading skirmishes into Angola. Raids across borders. Other expats had told me George boasted of audacious missions, crimes committed in blackface disguise in order to have deeds attributed to rebel liberation groups. I knew those experiences had shaped his point of view. But at this moment they were accusations and it seemed prudent to stay away from any of it.

George began to describe UN debates he'd been following on TV. Hours and hours of debates broadcast live on South African TV. George described details of investigations underway in the country. Names were being named. A truth commission was about to be convened.

*If George has been watching TV continuously,* I wondered, *how could he be working full-time?*

Apartheid was coming to an end and that meant George must be frightened. He began to defend, talking to me as if I was an interrogator.

He said, "There hasn't been one shred of evidence to support the view that there is army or police involvement."

I listened, but said nothing. There was too much to say. Every week new evidence appeared. Much of it pointed to army and police involvement.

Then George changed the direction of the conversation. "Have you seen the coverage of the Los Angeles riots?" He had watched CNN reports in Johannesburg. I had seen none of it although I knew about the incident following Rodney King's beating from reading *The Guardian*.

"The television coverage was amazing," he said. "Asian shop keepers with AK 47s firing at mobs from a balcony. I thought I was watching a revolution in South America."

There was nothing I could say. In the village, I had no chance of seeing TV news coverage. But his point was clear: civil disturbance, violence, takes place in your country, too.

We were interrupted by a cork popping in the kitchen. A special bottle of wine was opened. "Look, everyone," Ann announced. "New stem goblets. Plastic, but stem goblets all the same. From Jo'burg. Thank you, George . . .."

Already a tray of glasses was being brought around the room for a toast.

"None for me," Jim said loudly, his voice slurred. "I am boycotting South African wine." By this time, Jim had consumed countless cans of beer and was clearly drunk.

Marjorie's sketch pad lay closed on the seat beside her, she and Gen were still engrossed in conversation. They might have been the only two people in the room enjoying themselves.

Food was served shortly after Jim's proclamation. Turkey was not available, but roasted stuffed chicken with cranberries had been flown in from Jo'burg, along with the wine. Conversation continued after helpings were dished, and the room seemed to settle into a cozy hum.

Suddenly, I heard a crash and looked up.

George had lost control of his dish. His plate whirled crazily on the floor near his feet and all of his food had spilled. The plate itself was made of some unbreakable substance so there was no damage, but he bent over and cleaned up the mess, putting the food into the dog's dish then returning to lean in the doorway and sip his glass of wine.

"George, help yourself," Ann spoke in an even voice. "There's plenty more in the kitchen."

But George leaned into the wall hard enough to hold up a falling building. His face was red.

Ann looked at him steadily, her feet planted in the middle of the kitchen. *If you're going to have a tantrum, I'm not coming to the rescue,* she seemed to be saying.

He shook his head and held his ground.

Frank, sitting on the floor directly across the room, looked over at me. His plate in one hand, a goblet of red wine in the other, he lifted his glass and winked. *Not so bad, after all.*

BEFORE I COULD eat anything, I had to pause and breathe.

I closed my eyes for a second, blotting out the lecturing I had received, shutting out the accusations and defensiveness. Balancing my plate on my lap, I began to enjoy the familiar fragrances and was reminded it was not just the food that was familiar. Dipping my fork into the cranberry sauce, I remembered that this is Thanksgiving. In my mind I had a vision of dry corn stalks. I could almost feel the cool air, abundant food, and the coziness of a family gathering.

## Feast of Krishna

"WHY DO YOU THINK they invited us?"

Gen was as puzzled as I was.

"And for some reason it has to be today?"

The Ramasamys had asked us to come over for lunch, but neither of us understood why. This invitation was a complete surprise. For the entire two years we'd lived in the village we'd never socialized with them. Besides that, during the six months I had worked at the secondary school, Mr. Ramasamy and I had provoked and offended each other. Gen and I had tried to back out, but we didn't want to be rude and finally, we gave in.

Now, on this October 1992 day in Botswana, a month and a half before the end of our Peace Corps term, Gen and I walked to the Ramasamys' house on the grounds of the junior secondary school where she still taught. It was an easy walking distance and when we came to the gate at the school, I pushed it open.

Beyond the gate, a dusty driveway traced an arc between the school and a semicircle of concrete block teachers' houses — all of them, the same creamy yellow.

I had taught English at this school temporarily while my second-year students at the college were doing their practice teaching.

Across the drive I could see the top of the flagpole extending above the administrative building and it reminded me of the morning assemblies, when I stood with four hundred students and staff under that flagpole as daylight was just breaking in the eastern sky. I had fond memories of those mornings, the low slant of the sun's rays, the students singing hymns, and Ramasamy, a non-observant Hindu as far as I knew, stepping forward to read from a Gideon Bible he held in his hand. It seemed slightly humorous in those days, to see his expression of pious contemplation that made him look the part of a man from the London Missionary Society. He opened his Bible with a flourish to a marked page and announced, "My reading this morning is from Proverbs." Then, in a sonorous voice, he began to read:

My son, despise not the chastening of the Lord; neither
be weary of his correction:
For whom the Lord loveth he correcteth; even as a father
the son in whom he delighteth.
Happy is the man that findeth wisdom, and the man that
getteth understanding.

After reading the verse, complete with the "eth" endings on each verb, Ramasamy continued with his trademark self-serving interpretation, "Now, these words tell us that if your teacher scolds you or corrects you, he or she is helping you attain wisdom. You should welcome the words of your teacher. Even if she is scolding you, she does it out of love. Your teacher is helping you in your quest for wisdom and attainment in school. And, for those of you sent to my office . . ." — a nervous titter arose from the student body; everyone knew he referred to students sent to him for caning — ". . . remember that our job in my office is the same. I am only trying to help you gain understanding."

Next to the assembly grounds was the building that contained the staffroom. He and I had many conversations in that room, Ramasamy chain-smoking as we talked. Once, he asked me to witness a caning in his office, but I had a strong aversion to the process and I told him, "No."

He never asked me again and I was grateful for that. But afterward, a certain reserve entered into our relationship.

THE RAMASAMYS LIVED in the first house inside the gate, their yard precisely defined by a low chain-link fence. As Gen and I approached their home, I still wondered why I was there. I'd seen Ramasamy only once or twice since I left the secondary school. Whenever I saw him, I always greeted him, of course, with "Dumela," the usual greeting in this part of the world.

Near the front door, Ramasamy had installed a satellite antenna — a gray circular dish that was at least twelve feet in diameter. He was the only person in the village to own one and it took up much of his postage-stamp-sized lawn. Most people in the village kept grass out of their yards because it provided a potential hiding place for snakes. Ramasamy, however, had his grass delivered as chunks of sod and maintained his yard like a golf green. The only other lawn I'd seen in the neighborhood was at the college, where there was a small area planted with a type of tough green grass that never had to be mowed.

Along the fence, a neat row of pepper plants grew. Yellow, red, and purple chilies, all of them the size of small Christmas lights. Ramasamy offered me one once when I was teaching at the school; I took a bite and swore I'd never eat another. As soon as the chili hit my tongue, my eyes began to water and I thought I'd burst into flames. "Very healthful," he'd said at the time.

Ramasamy, a small man, quick and dark-skinned, greeted us as he stood inside his doorway. "Welcome. Come in," he said. He spoke with an accent that would have been difficult to place had he not described himself to me one time as a French-speaking Hindu Tamil from Mauritius.

Then, he announced, "It's an auspicious day!"

I didn't know what he meant by "auspicious" and didn't really want to ask. "Dumela," I said. Just outside the threshold, I extended my arm; we shook hands, distantly.

He was dressed casually in light-colored slacks. His blue shirt had a Hawaiian print with palm trees and flowers. I'd never seen him without a suit and cinched-up necktie. We entered the living room and Ramasamy led us to where a stuffed sofa was pushed against one wall near two facing chairs that made a conversation area. I could see Mrs. Ramasamy busy in her kitchen; she made a brief appearance to greet us.

"Do you need help?" Gen asked.

"Oh no, thank you," Mrs. Ramasamy said. "Everything is almost ready."

She was dressed for a special occasion, wearing a sari. She even wore a *bindi* — a decorative red dot between her eyebrows. It startled me to see her in a sari. Most days, she wore ordinary clothes. She was the only Indian woman I'd seen in Africa who wore jeans and a shirt. Many days when Gen and I walked by in the afternoon, we greeted her outside as she tended to her garden. She always seemed to have plenty of time to chat. I've seen photographs of Indian women at ceremonial occasions with flowers in their hair, wrists stacked with bracelets, rings on every finger. Today, other than her sari and bindi, she was unadorned and even in a sari, Mrs. Ramasamy was the same direct woman we had talked to in her yard.

After greeting us, she disappeared into the kitchen. A table between the living room and kitchen was arranged with plates and small bowls of various seeds for seasoning the food. At the center of the table, marigolds floated in a bowl.

Ramasamy, ushering us into the comfortable seating area, told us, "My wife has been working since early this morning preparing this special meal. This is an important day for us and she's cooking dishes we have only on holidays."

It was a Saturday in October. We weren't aware of any holiday. Gen and I were both wearing everyday clothes. "Peace Corps casual" was how we described the way we dressed in Africa. Gen in her teal-colored blouse and blue denim culottes, and me in my usual long-sleeved blue shirt and a pair of khaki trousers. Both of us wore once-upon-a-time white running shoes, now stained the color of red sand. I felt uncomfortable when I realized that the Ramasamys were dressed for a holiday.

I wondered if this special occasion had something to do with the fact that our Peace Corps term was ending and we'd be leaving the village soon, but as we made ourselves comfortable on the sofa, Ramasamy began telling us about the holiday — the Feast of Krishna. He told us that the day had its origins in the story of Rama — a reincarnation of Lord Krishna — who was looking for his wife, Sita. Sita had been kidnapped by a demon named Ravana.

"Today is the day," Ramasamy said, "that Rama is fighting Ravana the Demon. We have fasted for almost thirty days. Fasting purifies our bodies for the return of Rama next weekend when we celebrate Divali."

This was a much different kind of conversation than those I was used to having with him. Usually, Ramasamy was trying to gain the upper hand. This day, in his eagerness to share something about his culture, I heard a different quality in his voice — an openheartedness, perhaps.

He perched on the edge of his chair, as though ready to jump up at any time, telling us how he and his wife fasted and purified their bodies. "Our way of fasting is to eat vegetarian food. We eat traditional dishes and don't drink alcohol. Some people in our families are very strict vegetarians, but we are not. I don't see any reason for it, except before Divali."

AS HE SPOKE, I remembered how it was when we worked together at the school. Ramasamy, as deputy headmaster, had the responsibility for the school's dirty work — dispensing canings in his office, humiliating students on the school grounds, or assigning teachers to after school and weekend sports duties. It wasn't in his job description to be everyone's friend.

The low point in my relationship with him came after Gen returned home from school one day on the verge of tears, and when I asked, "What's wrong?" her face turned red and her body began to tremble.

"It's so unfair the way women are treated," she said. "I have the same teaching load as everyone else, yet I have to work this weekend because a sports team will be visiting for a match. Mr. Ramasamy says, 'They need to be fed.'" She spit out the words in an angry, mocking, high-pitched tone of voice. She hesitated for a moment, then shook both her fists and said, "Well, why the hell doesn't he cook for them?"

I didn't like it any more than she did.

The next day, Ramasamy and I had a discussion. I told him it was unfair — Gen worked as hard as any other teacher with a full weekly schedule, so why did she have to spend her entire weekend preparing meals for a sports team?

After our conversation he and I avoided each other until a few days later when he entered the staff room, took a seat and after lighting his cigarette, looked me in the eye. "The difference between Americans and me is cultural," he said. His necktie was spotless and cinched to the choking point. He wore an expensive suit in a soft green color. He paused, then told me, "I believe that life is a stage and we are all actors."

I'd been grading papers, but I set my things aside and gave him my full attention.

"Americans believe they need to feel guilty," he announced. "Ever since Adam and Eve got kicked out of the Garden of Eden, Westerners feel guilty about sin. I believe we're all actors." He jumped out of his chair, made a fierce grimace, and slashed the air with an imaginary sword, as if dealing a deathblow to an enemy. Amazingly, his cigarette was still intact. "We play our part and our job is to play it to the hilt!" He threw his hands into the air, "What's there to feel guilty about?" Then he laughed and gave a playful shrug. "If we play our parts we may argue. We may fight sometimes." He paused. "Sometimes people even fall in love."

My protests over Gen's weekend duties changed nothing. Whenever a weekend sports event was scheduled, forty or fifty athletes came to spend Saturday night in one of the classrooms and the responsibility to feed them continued to fall to the home-ec teachers.

IN HIS LIVING ROOM as Ramasamy continued to tell us the story of Rama trying to rescue Sita and fighting with Ravana, I couldn't help but remember my feelings that my wife had been kidnapped on those weekends she cooked for sports teams.

He told us a bit more of the background of the story, some of which I'd heard before. The details of Rama's quest for Sita, his ideal wife, was familiar to me. She is everything good and pure. Rama's fight with Ravana, the ideal villain, is a moral struggle, a triumph of good over evil. In some ways, it's a story about our virtuous selves struggling with our less virtuous nature.

Ramasamy said, "Divali is next week. The celebration of Rama's return when he brings Sita back home. It's a moonless night and the celebration takes place early in the morning in southern India, about 4:00 a.m. In northern India people celebrate after sunset with the festival of the lights. Lights are said to help guide Rama home to safety."

Gen spoke up, "Oh, this *is* an important day, isn't it? That's what you meant when you said it was auspicious. There must be millions of people who've fasted and prepared themselves for this day."

"That's right," he said. "In honor of the day, my wife has prepared a meal of several courses to serve you. All traditional dishes."

I was bowled over. Completely puzzled. Why would they invite *us* if it's such a special day in their culture?

At that moment, his wife invited us to the table. We seated ourselves and I smelled the fragrance of the marigolds in the center. It wasn't a sweet fragrance, but more of a freshened atmosphere around the table. I'd seen garlands of marigolds in photographs of shrines in India.

"The flowers are beautiful," Gen said. "Are they from your garden?"

"Yes. They are out of the yard," Ramasamy said. "These flowers are considered very auspicious. We use them on holidays." Then he added, "They help in overcoming obstacles."

Just then, his wife came out of the kitchen carrying a tray with two bowls of soup and two small plates with what looked to be some kind of relish. Ramasamy went into the kitchen and returned with a platter of Indian bread. On the table, his wife had placed a small cup of *ghee* — purified butter — for use on the bread, I assumed.

Ramasamy said, "This soup is *daal*. And this . . .," he said, pointing to the relish, a plate of shredded vegetables, mostly cucumber and bell pepper, ". . . is the salad. The bread, we call *naan*." He spoke almost like a tour guide explaining a new experience for novice visitors.

The daal was a rich golden color with green flecks of cilantro floating on the surface. The soup consisted of pureed lentils. The aroma of chilies, cumin, and other spices made my mouth water and gave advance notice, even before I'd had a taste, that it had plenty of heat.

"Everything in the dishes my wife has prepared promotes healing," he said. "Medicinally, the food is very beneficial."

*The food promotes healing!* The idea transformed the act of eating into a different kind of experience.

The daal was better than I imagined. Gen makes soup, of course, but the seasonings are different. If I "make soup," what I do is open a can. But the textures of the daal and the spices were a world away from anything I'd tasted. Mrs. Ramasamy had cooked the lentils herself. She'd added the seasoning and blended everything to perfection. Yogurt was on the table, as well as naan, rice, and the salad, all of which helped moderate the effect of the chilies. Spooning the daal, Gen and I tore off pieces of naan and savored the distinctive Indian seasoning. The salad had a mild cumin dressing that seemed to cool my tongue.

I became so immersed in the flavors in this first course, I almost overlooked the fact that the Ramasamys were not seated at the table. Gen and I were being served, while Mrs. Ramasamy tended to the food in the kitchen and her husband helped serve.

*There was something different going on here.* This meal was not an excuse to socialize. With each new course, Ramasamy gave us a lesson in his tour guide manner.

Gen looked up, as he set a steaming dish of vegetable *samosas* and a curry dip on the table. The fried pastry shells, triangular in shape, contained a filling of potatoes and vegetables. "Everything is so delicious," she said, loud enough for Mrs. Ramasamy to hear in the kitchen.

Just when I wanted to slow down and savor the banquet, Ramasamy brought another dish he called *chana masala* — spicy chickpeas with spinach and a curry seasoning. That was accompanied by a rice pilau — saffron rice, sautéed in butter. The blend of seasonings in the two dishes was unique. I'd never tasted anything like it. There was a subtle undercurrent of cinnamon, clove, and ginger. At the same time, the fragrance of onion, cardamon, and bay was overpowering.

Ramasamy perched briefly on the edge of a chair. "The spices in this meal are prescribed by *Ayurveda*, the science of life from ancient India," he said. "They promote digestion. Cinnamon is a mild stimulant and saffron in the rice has many medicinal properties. Other spices improve circulation and help the skin."

The idea of all this was intriguing. *Science of life from ancient India.* It was clear to me this meal meant more to our hosts than simply placing food on the table. Though I felt mildly skeptical of the medical claims, I enjoyed the aromas and the appearance of each dish. Also, the spices demanded attention in a positive way. Normally, I take seasonings for granted. This food required participation, with almost every bite I had to cool my palate with yoghurt, rice, or naan.

Ramasamy brought a small platter to the table and placed a dish in front of each of us. From where I was sitting, I couldn't see the food on the platter very well, but there was a lumpy whiteness — yoghurt, I assumed — with a garnish of green herbs. I was getting used to Ramasamy's descriptions. What would he say about the whiteness? I wondered. *Promotes purity? Cleansing?*

He spooned three balls on two small plates and may have intended to say something, but he was interrupted by a knock on the door.

"Very auspicious," Ramasamy said walking across the room to answer. "This is the best day of the year to feed people. When company comes on this day, it's as if God has sent them." He opened the door and two men entered, both tall and dressed in work clothes. It was their day off. He introduced them as friends from Mauritius.

After introductions, the conversation switched from English to French. The switch in language allowed Gen and me to eat in silence.

With a larger group to entertain now, Ramasamy went into the living room and switched on the TV. Thanks to his satellite dish he was able to flick through dozens of channels. He passed over a couple of English language stations from South Africa, then let out a yell. "Angola! You can't watch Angolan television," he yelled in disgust. "It's all in Portuguese!" *Apparently he considered that a sign of backwardness.*

Skipping on, he found a program in French. An audience of dignitaries were sitting before a flower-covered casket. The focus of the cameras was on the French president attending the funeral of a European leader.

Gen and I were served dessert — tea and two small bowls of spicy poached pears — and then it was time for the drop-in friends to be served. They continued conversing in French, talking over the noise of the television.

We then took a seat on the other side of the living room and I watched Ramasamy playing his role as host. Playing it to the hilt. In constant motion, he served the new guests at the table, then adjusted the volume on the TV. Trying to make everyone feel welcome, he carried on a conversation in French and addressed us in English. Finally, he walked over to a bookcase and pulled a videotape from the top shelf. "I taped the U.S. Presidential debates a couple of days ago," he announced and slid the tape into a VCR.

When the broadcast of the debates began, everyone's conversation switched to English and I felt more involved.

The new guests had followed the debates and news about the U.S. election in detail. They made statements and opinionated comments about American politics. Naively, I assumed they'd be interested in my opinion since I was an American. Yet, when I chimed in with a comment, or an interesting fact, their eyes glazed over. They sat in silence until I finished, then their conversation resumed.

Every time I felt the urge to say something, it was the same. They sat, waited politely, and didn't respond. It became a matter of great interest to me that I could induce a trance-like state in everyone just by opening my mouth. Finally, I stopped trying. I had a feeling the other men understood something about this occasion that I did not. They seemed to know I was not a friend, and therefore, felt no obligation to relate to me. But we were all riveted to the TV screen.

With the debate on TV, the banquet we had been served had a chance to settle, allowing a glow of satisfaction to rise up and spread through my body. While two men vied for the position of Leader of the Free World, I had a moment to think about Ramasamy's explanation about the day when people reenacted the story of Rama and Sita. Like Rama and Ravana, we have our struggles — obstacles to

overcome: difficult relationships, areas of our lives that require healing. And, like Sita, we all have something in our lives, true and good.

It made me wonder why I was here for this ritual meal. Did
Ramasamy want some kind of closure? Did he want to transform
negative aspects of our relationship before Gen and I left the village?
I had no answers. All I had were questions.

*Is the drama being reenacted now? In this room? Who is
Rama? Who is Ravana, the Demon? Or, are we taking turns,
each of us playing different parts?*

On the TV screen the debate ended and the two men who had
been arguing, rose from their chairs, walked toward one another and
shook hands. The two men at the dining table reacted immediately.
"Look at that!" said the first man. "The younger man has been insulting him for over an hour, yet they shake hands!"

"The most powerful man in the world!" the other said.

"Look, now their wives are coming on stage. In a circle . . . they
look like old friends."

"Standing there . . . smiling and chatting."

"How can he forgive those insults?"

I didn't try to say anything or contribute. I was still feeling a
pleasant glow from the meal and it began to translate into a kindly
feeling towards my host, Ramasamy. His effort to make his diverse
guests feel at home seemed extraordinary. I began to appreciate
what he was doing. Occasionally, I caught a glimpse of his wife as
she passed by the kitchen doorway and I felt grateful for her effort
in creating this meal.

Gen and I were effectively excluded from the conversation by
now. Neither of us had participated for a long while. We looked at
one another and some secret signal passed between us. In that silent
communication an agreement was achieved. It was time to thank
our hosts and take our leave.

## Staff Tea

COOKIES WERE NEVER SERVED at staff tea. At 9:30 in the morning teachers crowded into the staff room where there were chairs and soft seats, though nowhere near enough, and most of the lecturers and HODs — Heads of Department — stood in groups chatting, sipping tea, and snacking on biscuits.

In the US, cookies have always been synonymous with sweet pleasure. But in British usage a "cookie" refers to a chewy, rather tasteless kind of bread that accompanies bland or over salted soup.

When teachers at the Tonota College of Education in eastern Botswana, spoke of "biscuits" they meant something sweet, usually cream-filled and rich. In America, I would have called them "cookies." I found the reversal in meaning humorous, at first, and strange, since biscuits and cookies are opposites in my imagination. Biscuits, in my experience, were hard and chewy, and as a child, I never would have eaten one unless someone made me.

One person from among the teaching staff was designated to coordinate staff tea. His or her duties included plugging in two large electric urns of water each morning, setting out biscuits, and buying the tea bags, biscuits, and other supplies. Each teacher was expected to contribute to the tea fund, a monthly donation of five pula — equivalent to nearly $2.50 US.

Mid-month supplies dwindled and the entire staff was entertained by announcements from Dr. George Robertson, the Scotsman who coordinated staff tea for the college.

"May I have your attention, please," the announcement always began, the words chanted above all of the conversations echoing around the room. The words were followed by the tapping of saucers with teaspoons from various parts of the room as others attempted to help quiet the drone of conversation for his announcement.

Dr. Robertson had a thin trace of red hair and a booming voice. The top of his head was covered with spreading red sores from too much sun — only recently did he begin wearing a hat when he worked in the garden around his house. His announcements were delivered in the booming voice of an Anglican preacher, with the trilled r's and rounded tones of a sermon. Dr. Robertson, HOD Religion, also preached at the Anglican church in nearby Francistown.

"Sorry to interrupt," he would say, "but it is my sad duty to report that we are perilously close to running out of tea and biscuits for our morning gathering. There are members among us who have still not contributed for the month of October," implying that they hadn't contributed for November or December either. Every month Dr. Robertson made this announcement. "Very soon, I shall post names on the staff bulletin board. So please, do get your contribution to me as quickly as possible."

His manner always had the predictability and solemnity of a minister soliciting money from the pulpit for the purchase of hymnals, and his words were always followed by a murmur of nervous comments and jokes about those in arrears being struck by lightning or punished by God if they did not pay up. Dr. Robertson, himself, never registered any humor about the situation. He was doing his duty and would continue to do so. Others may do what they wish.

As soon as he had finished his little speech, he turned immediately and busied himself with straightening boxes of tea bags or counting his remaining inventory.

Most teachers on the staff gravitated to conversation groups at staff tea according to language, nationality, or tribal affiliation. Zambians discussed politics in Zambia. Zimbabweans conversed among themselves about the military situation at home. Often, among the Zimbabweans, the MaShona or the N'debele separated themselves in order to speak their own language. Batswana on the staff conversed among themselves in circles that were loud and frequently punctuated by bursts of laughter.

As the only American on the staff, I found myself in the position of having to circulate in order to find conversation. Sometimes, I sat in a circle with the British and Rhodesians — white-skinned teachers and HODs — all of whom spoke English. I felt uncomfortable, however, sitting in what felt like a racially segregated grouping. Usually, I would circulate and talk to as many people as I could.

During staff tea, I got to know several teachers from Uganda. The Ugandans spoke several languages, Swahili, at least two tribal languages, and excellent English. I found them urbane and interested in talking to me about African culture. Like many of the teachers on the staff, each of them straddled two cultures. In Uganda they had close links with their own villages and in their professional lives they all functioned in an educational and institutional environment defined by British custom.

My next door neighbor, whom I knew as John, sat among this group. He had a Ugandan name which was, he told me, completely unpronounceable for Westerners. So, for two years, I knew him only as John.

JOHN WAS TALL, in his mid twenties, and his skin was a rich black color. His thin face and straight prominent nose gave him almost a European appearance. Except for his neatly groomed black hair and skin color, John had none of the other features that seem to define Africans.

My first impressions of him were formed when we both came to this village and to this college, on the same day, two years earlier riding in the back of a three-ton cattle truck.

I remember that at the end of a long day of travel, three of us remained in the vehicle. It was uncomfortable to sit, so my wife and I stood trying to maintain our balance in spite of the rolling and pitching on the sandy roads. That day, John stood in a stiff-legged posture wearing a checkered suit coat, dark slacks, a white shirt, and tie. The formality of his clothing in the back of a livestock truck seemed incongruous and his manner, rigid and formal.

There had been seventeen of us in the truck when it turned off the tarred highway and into the village of Tonota. There were Peace Corps teachers, teachers assigned by the British Council, and teachers coming from other African countries assigned by the Botswana Ministry of Education — all of us to work here on the eastern edge of the Kalahari Desert.

Along the way we made stops at schools throughout the sprawling community dropping off teachers at their assignments, as our truck bumped over the rutted dirt road headed for the final stop at the Tonota College of Education eight kilometers from the main highway.

For the last two kilometers, the road dwindled to a sandy track and the truck made slow progress as it had to stop and slow down frequently making way for cattle, goats, or burros.

During this last part of the journey, John, alone in the truck with us two Americans, had become painfully silent. I imagined that our backgrounds were so different, he did not see any way of bridging the distance. Or, maybe he did not see any need. Once or twice, I tried to initiate a conversation, and he would nod and respond with a one syllable, "Umm."

For me it was a lark to be bouncing up a dirt road in the back of a truck. Each of the three of us was a long ways from home. Though

I knew next to nothing about him, I could imagine the weight that this assignment had for him. He was a new teacher getting established in a new country, and, like other expatriate African teachers, he would be planning to send money home to support his parents and extended family.

Late that afternoon, the truck finally turned into the drive leading to a paved parking lot near the administrative offices of the college.

"This must be where you are headed," I said to him.

He didn't respond verbally, but only raised his eyebrows and flickered a silent, "Yes," with his eyes.

The truck stopped in front of a college building and the representative from the Ministry of Education climbed down out of the cab and walked into the administrative offices. John climbed out of the truck and waited on the asphalt surface. I remember the sight of him looking lonely and frightened, as he stood in the parking lot holding all of his worldly belongings, a blanket, a thin briefcase, and a clear plastic bag with a plate, knife, fork, and spoon.

The representative returned to the truck accompanied by the deputy principal of the college, an older African man, tall and paunchy. The eyes of the deputy principal were round and prominent and when he looked at any of us his eyes seemed to burn with intensity and aggression.

In my previous work at schools and colleges I had learned that the "number two," the deputy in this case, was a person assigned to perform the unpleasant chores at the institution. They have acquired the skills that allow them to be aggressive or even nasty, and often they display a thick-skinned attitude as a form of professional certification.

In that situation John's face remained completely impassive. He showed no visible signs of emotion. I had to reassess my impression that he was frightened. Instead, I saw indications of John's inner reserve and competence as he handled every challenge the deputy raised and the deputy wasted no time on pleasantries.

"Are you sure you belong here?"

John answered every challenge with his cultured British accent, the best defense against surly bureaucrats.

The deputy seemed to toy with John that afternoon. He implied that he doubted a man as young as John could teach anything at the college level. He doubted that John had the credentials.

But John answered all of the deputy's doubts and to the question of his having the credentials, he informed the deputy that he'd graduated from Oxford the previous June.

Still, the deputy seemed prepared to send John back to the Ministry of Education in Gaborone.

Finally, the deputy told him, "I suppose the thing to do is to give you housing, at least for the weekend. I'll call the driver Monday to take you, if need be."

That afternoon, I'd watched the two men walk away from the truck, the deputy moving with John in tow, his belongings under each arm, appearing to be a man lost in the wrong end of Africa.

IT TOOK GEN AND ME two weeks to get permanent housing at the teacher's college, and by coincidence, our new house turned out to be next door to John's. In the two weeks since I had seen him, he'd become involved with a beautiful young Motswana woman.

The first time I saw them together they looked very much in love. She was lighter than John, her apricot skin glowed in his presence and her round dark eyes seemed to see no one else.

Because John was so totally involved with his girlfriend, we never had a conversation over the hedge that divided our yards. He and I spoke to one another only in the staff room. I found him to be a very serious young man. Once I tried to create humor out of our typical morning greeting in the staff room, "Hi, John." "Hello, John." It was immediately obvious that he did not think it was humorous to make light of another person's name and I gave up the effort.

Like the other Ugandans I knew on the staff, John was fascinated by American culture. Much of our conversation consisted of me answering questions about something outrageous that he had read about America.

Those conversations often began the same way, with John saying, "My God, John, what's going on in America, anyway?"

One day at tea, he produced an international edition of *Newsweek* from under his arm. On his face he had a bemused expression. He held up the magazine so I could see the cover. What I saw was a feature headline proclaiming a men's movement in America.

"I haven't seen the story," I told him. "What does it say?"

"Well, it talks about men going into therapy groups and then getting together in the woods to dance and beat drums. It all sounds so bizarre. Why would people want to go back to beating drums . . . in the most technologically advanced nation in the world? Primitive behavior."

When he said, "Primitive behavior," he said it in a way that made it sound as if he was describing the "End of civilization as we know it."

I couldn't think of a way of explaining that would make any sense. Problems of men's identity. Roles of men and women in the US. Where would I begin?

"Can't tell you what it's about, I guess."


IN MID-DECEMBER, a memo was distributed to the faculty announcing that I was leaving the college in a week and my teaching contract in Botswana was coming to an end.

The next day, John came to talk to me at staff tea.

When he approached me that morning, I expected him to say goodbye.

"It looks as if I will be leaving, as well, John."

I was stunned, and remembering his girlfriend, I said, "I thought you would be staying, John."

"No, I have to go home. I have just received word that my parents have arranged a marriage for me."

John was visibly devastated.

The idea of him giving up everything — his job, his girlfriend — sounded preposterous to me.

"But, John, do you really have to do that. Don't you have some say in the matter? It's your life, after all. Your career."

John seemed deliberate and rational in his explanation. He knew his duty.

"It would be destructive for me to simply go against my parents' wishes. No. I couldn't do that. I will have to leave."

In his hand he held a thin China saucer gracefully, between thumb and forefinger. A cup of tea and a small teaspoon balanced on the saucer. A biscuit with a sweet creamy center leaned precariously on the edge.

"It means a lot of changes in my life. I do feel a certain amount of turmoil."

He took a small bite of his biscuit. It was a dutiful bite. A formality. His expression reflected distaste rather than enjoyment. His shoulders slumped and his face became impassive.

"Quit my job . . . move back to Uganda . . .."

As he summarized his duties, he sipped his tea. His face betrayed no sign of emotion.

"Get married . . .."

His cup made a loud clink as he planted it firmly back on the saucer.

"I'll have to break up with my girlfriend."

# Elsie's Village

GEN AND I HAD BEEN making contact with the *San* people (Bushmen) in the Kalahari Desert and talking to them to learn whatever we could about their lives. In the last week of our time in Botswana we made a detour to the west in our rental truck to Lehututu because it was the place where our friend, Elsie, had grown up. She had talked enthusiastically about her village in our conversations and told us we ought to visit there before we leave the country. Since we were driving in the western Kalahari and both of us were curious, why not?

ELSIE WAS ONE OF THE FIRST PEOPLE I met when I started teaching at the college in eastern Botswana. The first day faculty came together, someone told her that I was an American and so she made a point of introducing herself. "I was in America last year," she said to me.

Elsie was a tall, beautiful woman, her skin like shiny copper, and she had just returned from a year's sabbatical, earning a master's degree from the University of Minnesota. In the college staff room with a cup of tea in her hand, glowing with good humor, she told me about living in Minneapolis. "As you would expect, everything was different there," she said. Her eyes twinkled as we talked and I could feel the infectious quality of her outgoing friendliness. "Winter was harsh; the food was very strange. I was the only black person for miles around and although people were friendly, everyone stared. I felt like a celebrity."

She took a sip of her tea. "My apartment was near the river and one day I stopped at a nursery to see if I could buy a flowering plant for my small room and I found one. I had never seen a plant like it. Full of beautiful red flowers, and the moment I saw it, right away I knew it was just what I wanted for my drab apartment. On my way home from the nursery, I crossed the bridge and balanced it on my head." Elsie gave a slight shrug. "You know, the easiest way to carry it. So, walking across the bridge I carried it African-style back to my apartment. But the reaction of other people was shocking. It was late afternoon, rush hour, and cars stopped — traffic didn't move at all — everyone just wanted to watch."

I could imagine the picture. A statuesque woman carrying a potted indoor plant by balancing it on her head. Not something you see every day in the U.S.

Elsie had a distinct appearance among the other Africans, too, different from the other faces in the college staffroom. She was tall, but her face seemed out of proportion for her size. Her face was too small and she had sharply delineated cheekbones that reminded me of the San people — the Kalahari Bushmen.

Elsie told me she had been born in the west, near the Namibian border, and was raised in a village called Lehututu. The college where we both taught was on the eastern edge of the desert, and, at the time, I'd not traveled to that area.

"What's it like there?" I asked.

"Aiyy! Impossible to say in words what's it like. You have to see it for yourself."

DURING THE FOLLOWING MONTHS, Elsie frequently approached me in the staff room to tell me something she had thought of or to give me a clipping about the people in the desert. In newspaper articles, the people of the western Kalahari were often referred to with a bureaucratic acronym, RADs, Remote Area Dwellers.

Elsie's people were the Bakgalagadi. "The language is similar to Setswana, but its roots, I believe, are in Zulu. My ancestors came to the Kalahari to escape war or slave trading in the south during the time of King Shaka Zulu, at least that's my belief. The people that live in Lehututu came from the south, nobody knows when, but probably about 180 years ago."

"When the people arrived did they move into land that was empty?" I asked.

"Oh no," she said. "When they came the Kalahari was already populated."

"Who lived there?"

"The Bushmen. They've lived in the Kalahari since forever. But, what I wanted to tell you is the language is different from the Tswana — close but different. The language has definite similarities with Zulu. When the people arrived, they intermarried with the Bushmen and Tswana. Of course, that's a way to bring peace when different people come together. Intermarriage. Water is scarce in the Kalahari and everyone needs to live near a waterhole. It's better to live in peace."

I asked her about the word Kalahari. "What does the word mean?"

"Nobody knows what the word means. I don't know where it comes from. Usually people say it means land of great thirst." The main thing Elsie wanted me to know was that it was not just a dry, brown, rolling land leading from one empty space to another. "There are more people than you would think. More animals. Variety."

TWO YEARS LATER, when our Peace Corps service was nearing completion, I told Elsie that Gen and I were making plans to travel through the Kalahari.

Elsie's niece, a student who had been in my class, was a small woman and quite shy. When I told her I was going to travel to Lehututu, surprisingly she became quite excited, and came to my office to talk to me about the village.

I took a map from my desk, unfolded it and pointed to Lehututu. I said, "It must be very dry there."

She hesitated as though the thought had never occurred to her, "Yes, it is dry," she agreed finally, "but the people are happy there. We live happily, we have our friends and family there." Then, so I would be even more interested in traveling to Lehututu, she added an interesting fact. "It is a place where people can cook without fire," she said, and added, "After a hunt, or when a goat is slaughtered, the meat is cut into strips and dried over a rack. The dried meat is called *biltong*."

ONCE WE WERE ON THE ROAD driving across the Kalahari Desert both Gen and I thought about Elsie. I was always aware of this as the place where Elsie was born, a place she loved.

A Peace Corps friend named Jack supervised an organization known as the Brigades, the trade and technical school for the region. When we arrived in Lehututu we had trouble finding the school where Jack said we could set up our tent.

It was becoming dark, and I began to get nervous about finding the Brigades. Near a primary school, I stopped at the teacher housing to ask directions.

A friendly woman, who was a teacher at the school, came out of her home with her nine-year-old daughter and introduced herself as Doris. When I asked her for directions, she made a map in the air with her hands and with her right hand showed me how the main road twisted and, finally, she gestured where we should turn left.

"Stay on the road," Doris said as her hand showed the path the road followed, "stay on the road," another squiggle in the air. "Turn left, you will see a building that has no roof. That's supposed to be a tannery. Another building with unfinished walls. It's supposed to be a shop."

I thanked her and followed her directions until we found the place.

Friday morning, we were sitting on our log stools making tea on our little butane camp cooker when the construction crew showed up for work. I asked about Jack. "Is he around?"

"He's gone. In Gaborone." Fortunately we got permission from the contractor to stay where we were — over the weekend at least.

ELSIE HAD RECOMMENDED that I contact her cousin, a man I should talk to in Lehututu. According to her, he knew a lot about the village. The place to find out where he lived was at the *kgotla*, the offices that form the village center. I drove there and parked the truck under a large shade tree so that the truck would be as cool as possible for Gen, who had decided to let me pursue an authority on Lehututu.

There was a pole fence nearby marking the meeting area for the villagers. Behind the fenced area were two concrete block buildings. They were obviously buildings where official business was done.

As I approached, two men came walking out of one of the buildings. One was wearing a tan safari suit, open at the collar. He looked at me and saw that I had a question. Taking the hand of the other man he led him towards me, and saying "Sala sentle," he took his leave. He was obviously the other man's boss or superior.

The underling found himself standing in front of an inquisitive white man. He said, "*Ga ke bue Sekgoa.*" (I don't speak English.)

I told him in Setswana that I was looking for a house. I told him the name. A look of relief came over his face and he pointed toward a group of houses that stood half a mile away. "The yellow one," he replied.

We drove through deep sand to get there. Except for the yellow house, all the houses in the group were traditional mud houses with thatched roofs. A hedge grew along the narrow drive, and there was a gate in the middle. I entered the gate, walked to the door, and called out, "*Koko.*" (The equivalent of knocking on the door.)

There was no answer.

I walked around the house and found three women doing laundry in a far corner of the yard. I greeted them and tried to explain in Setswana, "I am an American and I am looking for someone who can tell me about the village of Lehututu. When I return to America I will write about the village and tell others about the place."

My Setswana grammar was not perfect. One of the women scrubbing clothes on a washboard, watched me disapprovingly, then muttered to the others, "He says 'wrote.' He will 'wrote' about the village. If the white man can't talk, how can he write?"

The oldest woman in the group was sitting on a checkered blanket in the sand. "Mmm. Ehe, mma," she said, agreeing as she listened.

Then she turned and addressed me politely. There was a formality in her manner and she seemed to take me in with a directness, her dark eyes set in deeply-wrinkled cheeks. After we talked, she turned and spoke to the third woman, who was younger and possibly the wife of the man I wanted to see, asking her to go find someone for me to talk to. The young woman obliged and hurried across the yard to a neighboring compound.

In time, the man she had summoned walked into the yard. "The person you want to see is in Gaborone, but someone at the village office can help. The *kgosi* is in today," he said, referring to the village chief.

WHEN I ARRIVED BACK at the kgotla, a man greeted me as he walked out the gate I was about to enter. He was a broad-shouldered man about 5 feet 8 inches tall. He looked at the rental truck sitting under the shade tree. On the door was a yellow sign that read "Hertz–Safari Class."

"Hmmph, 'safari,'" he said. The thought of someone on safari in Lehututu made no sense. He became instantly disdainful.

"Yes, a rental truck," I said, pointing to the vehicle. Since I knew he could speak English, I explained my mission.

He pointed to the offices behind him, "Someone in there can help, I am sure."

I entered and found five offices inside, signs on the doors explained who was supposed to occupy each office, Village Chief, Sub Chief, Land Board, and two unmarked. But the offices were all empty. Outside one of the offices, a young man sat waiting on a bench. I asked him where these people were.

He got up and led me the way I had come. Pointing out the man I had just spoken to, now standing in the shade of a tree talking to two young men. "He is the kgosi."

I sauntered back to where the man stood.

"Dumela." I said.

"*Gape.*" (Hello, again.)

"Are you the kgosi?"

"Yes." A look of resignation crossed his face.

I introduced myself, and he told me his name was Mr. K. M. Leswape. We chatted briefly and very quickly the conversation turned to the lack of rain and the fact that a lot of cattle had died in the drought. "Have you seen rain anywhere else?" he wanted to know. "There still is no rain here and no grass for the cattle. We've had a mere sprinkle in the last week."

"Yes. I think the rain has followed us," I said. "In Maun, Dkar, and Ghanzi. It hadn't rained for two years in Ghanzi, but it poured the last two nights we were there." *It crossed my mind that I was suggesting a magical connection.* The kgosi seemed unimpressed.

"I am on my way to another village," he said. "Waiting for a truck, so I don't have long to talk. The truck will be here soon."

Before he left, the kgosi said, "If you want to know exactly how much rain we have had, see Mr. Sento, the head teacher at the elementary school. They have the village rain gauge at the school."

I WENT BACK to the truck and Gen was having a conversation with a young man doing his national service in the village. The purpose of national service in Botswana is to familiarize young people with the different cultures and tribal groups in their own country. He was from another part of the country and staying with a family in Lehututu. He had been living there for only a month.

Since his tribe was Bangwaketse, from southern Botswana, he was still getting used to the way people speak in the Kalagadi District. As I approached, he was telling Gen, "In my village, we say 'good morning,' 'O tsogile jang?' They say, '*Wa dzoha*' here. It sounds funny." He said it without any tone of mockery. "When they say, good afternoon, they say, '*O rele.*' In my village that means 'you have something on your head.' It's so strange."

It was surprising to him that people did not speak the same way.

"The people here are not developed," he said. "They draw their water from wells. In my village we use the tap."

GEN AND I THEN DROVE over to the primary school. I wanted to find the head teacher, Mr. Sento. School was out and most of the teachers had left.

When I found his house, I walked into Mr. Sento's yard and called, "Koko."

A young woman was working in the garden on the other side of the house. She appeared around the corner.

"Mr. Sento?" I asked.

"*O teng.*" (He's here.)

I waited on the doorstep while she went into the house and left the front door open. As she disappeared into a back bedroom, I could see the pictures on the living room walls. All of them were pictures of Jesus Christ. In a large-framed reproduction of the Last Supper, Christ and the disciples were all white-skinned.

Mr. Sento came to the door and shook hands with me. He looked sleepy. I introduced myself. "Yes," he said.

"I am interested in information about Lehututu and the people of the village."

"Yes," he said.

"Earlier in the day, I talked with Kgosi Leswape."

"Yes."

"He suggested that I try to talk with you, since you have lived in the village for a long time." In actual fact, the kgosi had said Mr. Sento would know how many millimeters of rain had fallen. But references are helpful.

"Yes," he said again.

I could tell this was not going to be an easy conversation. "Can you tell me where the Bakalahadi come from?"

The question was one that he was apparently well prepared for. He gathered his poise and seemed to be lecturing to his primary pupils. "Well, as I have been taught . . .," he said to me, or to his imaginary class, full volume, speaking precisely, "The people came to the village in the early 19th century. Their tribal name means 'people who have run away without permission.'"

"Why did the people leave the land in Lesotho and South Africa?"

"To escape the Zulu wars, of course."

By this time, we had moved into his small living room and were seated in a circle of overstuffed furniture, everything upholstered in green. A coffee table with a green checkered table cloth crowded our legs.

The conversation continued, and after each of his answers to my questions, Mr. Sento seemed to regard me with suspicion.

"Well, Mr. Sento, thank you for taking the time."

"Yes."

It felt impossible to extract myself. The conversation had no momentum and the two of us sat, stuck in our inertia. Probably my fault for not thinking this through more carefully. I did not know how to end it and neither did he.

"How long has your school been here in Lehututu?" I asked.

His eyes rolled up to look at the ceiling. "Since 1926," he said. "And, of course, before that it was a missionary school."

"How long have you been the head teacher?"

He looked at me proudly, "I came here in 1986."

I congratulated him on his long tenure. "That's a long time. When did you start teaching?"

"I started teaching in 1960."

"Really! You know I started teaching in 1961. We started in almost the same year."

There began to be a glimmer, a spark, of rapport. He smiled proudly and volunteered a list of villages where he had taught, Ghanzi, and Hukuntsi in the west of the country, Bokspits, and some in South Africa, and he mentioned a few others. He seemed relieved to know, also, that he had at least one year of seniority over me.

We had chatted about the schools and villages for a while when I started to excuse myself once more, but then I asked one more question, "Do you have any Basarwa [San people in Setswana] children at your school?"

His suspicion had begun to melt, but once more his facial expression adopted a look of infinite patience. "Oh yes. My little Basarwa children do very well. They get As. They come here for the upper level primary grades — five, six, and seven. They used to run away, but we have made changes and now they all feel settled."

"Where do they come from?"

"They come from the settlements in the district — Make, Monong, Ncang. They board here at the school during the week."

"What changes have you had to make at the school to help them 'feel settled'?"

"Well, I don't punish them. If I am nice they feel settled. No matter what they do, I don't punish them."

I had a strong feeling that this was a rehearsed performance. I guessed that he'd been asked these same questions by field workers from the Ministry of Education.

"If they tear a book, I say, 'Oh don't tear the book. Where will you get information?' If they smoke, even though they are small, I don't treat them harshly. 'Oh, my little friend, don't you know that if you smoke, it will damage your growth?'

"Basarwa children do well in class. Especially in science. They all know the trees, the edible plants, the spoor of animals. They could teach those things to the other students. They do well in science. The only subject they don't do well in is math. There is something wrong with their thinking."

Our interview ended with Mr. Sento giving me a lesson comparing English, Setswana, and Sekalahadi. I rose from my overstuffed chair and he walked out to the truck with me. I opened the driver's side door and he said, "Farewell."

I drove away with a feeling that I could not trust much of the information Mr. Sento had provided, especially about the Basarwa children.

SATURDAY MORNING I woke up at 6:00 a.m. with the sound of rain sprinkling lightly on the tent. I stayed in my sleeping bag listening to the rain, then fell back asleep. It was 7:30 when I finally crawled out of the tent. We had time to move slowly and rest today. I set about preparing a four-course breakfast on our single burner stove: a cup of tea, a boiled egg, a piece of toast, and a second cup of tea.

At 9:30 with my second cup of tea in my hand, I started sorting out notes and collecting my observations. I spent most of that day working on notes. Occasionally, Gen and I fired up the stove and had another cup of tea together. Later, I cleaned the tent and sorted out things in the truck.

It was a perfect morning with an overcast sky and a cool breeze. If the sky had been clear, the day would already be too hot. The sprinkling of rain during the night had cooled the air.

In the afternoon the weather seemed to tease the village. Clouds covered the sun and the sky turned black. We could see lightning and we heard thunder. We even smelled the rain. A few drops fell on the village. Then the clouds vanished and the afternoon became a scorcher.

I was feeling at a loss because I had not been able to meet Elsie's cousin. I was sure that a conversation with him might have been more rewarding than the one I had with Mr. Sento.

Late in the day, Gen and I walked around the village, I still wished I could meet someone who knew Elsie. We returned to camp to cook dinner. We placed our carved log stools where we could lean back against the porch of our friend's empty unfinished house. From our perch, we watched the sunset and the clouds build up in the west, over the Namibian border. Thunderheads flashed with lightning, mostly too distant for us to hear the sound of thunder. Clouds converged and built up all around us. In every direction we saw a show of flashing light. Occasional distant rumbles carried across the desert. In a circle, directly overhead, the sky became clear and as the night grew darker, the stars grew brighter. We sat entranced by the display in the heavens. The beauty was immense and it gave me a breathless feeling as the black, flashing, starry universe revolved above us.

Sunday morning we left the village and driving on the dusty road we passed women carrying water on their heads. The sight made me think of Elsie carrying her potted plant across the bridge in Minneapolis.

Along the way we picked up a hitchhiker. The young man was a teacher doing his national service at the Make settlement for the San. He taught in the primary school there. I asked him how the children fare at school. "The Basarwa children find school difficult," he said. "The culture is so different and the language causes trouble since they have to speak Setswana at school."

The young teacher spoke with directness and honesty. He seemed sensitive to the difficulties the children faced. Then he said, "Many of them never even heard Setswana until they came to our school. Their best subject is math."

I trusted his words, and driving away from the village where Elsie grew up, I realized that I felt good. I had confidence in this young man.

# Lunch in Lusaka

AFTER OUR TEACHING JOBS in Botswana ended with the completion of our Peace Corps service, Gen and I took the long way home. We camped in the Kalahari for a month. In Zimbabwe we hitchhiked in order to revisit some favorite places, and then crossed the border into Zambia at Victoria Falls.

We knew ahead of time that Zambia was going to be a problem for us. The economy had tanked and people were desperate, but a brief stop in Lusaka was necessary because we needed to get visas for Tanzania and Kenya, which we thought would be a simple matter of paying the fees and getting two stamps in our passports. Two . . . three days at the most, right?

Wrong!

It was on a Monday that we left our passports at the Tanzanian Embassy to get visa stamps. Two days were needed for the clerk to put a stamp on the page.

We next went to the Kenyan Embassy. Their visa process was supposed to take one day, but it stretched to three because the woman whose job it was to carry the passport to the clerk's desk had a sick child. When we returned to the Kenyan Embassy for the third time, hoping that our visas were ready, a clerk informed us that, "Documents will not be available until Friday afternoon."

Initially we stayed in a high-priced hotel in Lusaka near the bus station. At that hotel we discovered that we were using the same towels used by the previous guests, the room was never cleaned, and the beds were never made.

Finally, on Saturday, we moved to a shabby hostel that another traveler had told us about that was at least affordable. Following her directions, we walked down Burma Road; there was hardly any automobile traffic. At Nationalist Road, we found a red dirt path that led us under a long row of purple blooming jacaranda and fragrant flame trees with brilliant orange blossoms. When we arrived at the hostel, we found that it had a whitewashed brick wall surrounding the compound. A plaque at the gate read "YWCA Hostel." Just to the left was a sign stenciled in green on the white brick; "NO URINATING" it said. As we picked our way across the dirt entrance path, we avoided the worst of the mud puddles, but could not avoid the ironic strong smell of urine.

The reception window was dark, but handwritten signs taped to the brick wall around the window answered questions for potential residents. That was where we learned the price of a room was 3,200 *kwacha*. I did a quick calculation — the equivalent amount in U.S. dollars was roughly $4.75 per day. That was better than the hotel where we had been paying $90 for a dirty room.

We tracked down the manager of the hostel and she introduced herself as Christina. I liked her immediately. She greeted us with a wide smile and a kind gaze. A large woman with skin the color of light coffee, her graying hair emphasized her dignity. Christina wore three wide ivory bracelets on each arm and she told us, "The bracelets are my connection to my tribe."

"We have only one room available for a married couple," Christina said as she led us into an open-air courtyard. Just off the courtyard, she opened a door into a dank cell. Gen and I stepped inside. Vines that grew over the outside of the building covered the only window. A bare bulb hanging from the center of the ceiling provided the source of light. Two squeaky, sagging, army-style metal cots shoved against opposite walls left a three foot gap in the middle of this matrimonial suite.

Christina adopted the role of house-mother to inform me that as a male guest, I could use the shower between the hours of ten and noon, after the young women in the hostel had left for their jobs.

We had no better options.

We brought our bags from the hotel and moved in later the same day. Within a few minutes after sitting down on our cots for the first time, we heard the brief roar of a drenching tropical rain pour into the open courtyard. Then we watched the water seep under the door of our room.

At that point Gen's normally sunny disposition disappeared. She began to take things personally.

"How long do you think we'll be here?" she asked.

"Next train is Tuesday." I tried to sound positive, "That's only four days."

Our plan was to travel onward to Dar-es-Salaam, a two-and-a-half day train ride to the east coast of Africa.

"Four days," she said. "I don't know if I can make it."

"Well, our belongings are safe here." I sat on the edge of my cot and opened my bag, then began sorting through rumpled clothing. "The people are friendly. It's a place we'll meet other travelers . . . our best chance to get to know Zambians."

"Four days feels like a jail sentence." She sat on her metal cot opposite and I heard her suck in a deep breath. "This room is as dirty as anything I've ever seen. I can stay here for four days. Not a day longer!"

Gen's eyes had a dull appearance and I could tell this was a traumatic experience, and of course, I was concerned. She and I

213

were loving companions and good friends. I'd seen her like this once before in Peace Corps training. We'd been plunged into our cultural orientation, language instruction, and teacher training, and it became overwhelming for her at one point. Tensions were high and she had what she still refers to as a "mini-breakdown." It lasted three or four hours. She came out of it and became a dedicated teacher.

In the hostel cell, I resisted the urge to try talking her out of the way she felt as I knew arguing would be futile. Instead, I made a show of moving in. As she spoke, I wanted to demonstrate that the place was all right. I stacked my laundry on my cot, then with clean clothes in my hand, opened a drawer in the small dresser at the foot of my bed.

Immediately, I put everything back in my duffel bag and Gen watched quietly as I inspected the dresser. Then I began pulling drawers out of the chest and carried them into the courtyard.

"What's the matter?" she asked, when I came back to the room.

I crinkled my nose. "You don't want to know." Without another word I dragged the entire chest out of the room.

Gen was sitting up straight now and could see the squirming, crawling cluster of cockroaches in the back of the chest. In every corner, roaches huddled in the cracks.

Just then, the manager entered the courtyard.

"Christina," I called. "We've got an infestation here. Is there something we can do?"

"Oh, dear," Christina bent over to look. "I'll say. Leave everything here. I'll take care of it."

I went into the room and zipped my duffel. "I think I'll leave stuff in my bag."

"Me, too," Gen said. "I don't want to unpack."

Within minutes, Christina returned, shaking an aerosol can in her hand. The black and green label proclaimed "Doom."

We went back to our room. I closed the door behind us, but the smell of roach killer wafted through the open transom.

Later that day, we took a long walk in the warm rain. We didn't know anything about the neighborhood, but soon we found ourselves in an area of walled compounds and large mansions. Every car we saw seemed to be a black Mercedes limousine. We'd taken other long walks in Lusaka while tending to details at the embassies, but never into this district. We turned on Addis Ababa Road, a mile from the hostel, and walked near a lush, green lawn with tropical plantings, a park-like area with beautifully maintained trees and shrubbery. The landscaping suggested luxury, pampering. A sign by a paved driveway announced, "Pamodzi Hotel and International Restaurant."

"Hungry?" I asked. I looked at Gen, but my question had not registered in her mind. She seemed to be in a state that allowed only the endurance of pain. Normally, she'd jump at the chance for a meal in a luxury hotel. Today, she was like an impoverished child outside a candy store, her nose pressed to the glass, but convinced that any delights inside were beyond her means.

I took her by the hand and led her through the door. "C'mon, let's take a look at the menu."

Inside, the Pamodzi was everything that the hostel was not. Orderly. Clean. The dining room was fragrant with fresh coffee and steaming curry.

We took seats among other international travelers, businessmen, and government officials. A waitress approached our table with efficient steps and gave us each a menu and asked if we would like drinks. Shortly she returned with two bottles of beer while we made our selections.

We took our time, paging carefully, turning each page together as if we were reading each other a fairy tale bedtime story. Each page of the menu listed a different cuisine. German, French, and English dishes. Indian curries. On every turn of the clean colorfully-decorated pages, we deliberated. Gen's eyes now opened to the possibilities. We could order anything we wanted!

"Look, they serve hamburgers!" she cried.

When our order arrived, the hamburgers were served on a platter heaped with French fries. With steaming food on the table before us, there was a reverent moment, then we lifted glasses of Zambian lager to our good fortune.

With our burgers stacked with fresh lettuce, tomatoes, and onions, and our French fries liberally dowsed with ketchup, we were transported away from the embassy hassles. We could forget the clerks who took three days to carry our papers from one desk to another. Here, we were no longer dealing with an infestation of cockroaches. Across the table, Gen's eyes sparkled.

It was comfort food in the Pamodzi and, not only that, from our table we looked out a window onto a hanging garden with water spilling down a rockery into a pool of golden carp. Tropical flowers surrounded the pool and brightly colored birds flitted about.

A guilty pleasure. How long had it been since we'd been served anything but goat knuckles, greasy chicken wings, or curry with ingredients we didn't dare inquire about? But we considered ourselves mature adults and neither of us wanted to admit how completely we were allowing ourselves to be taken in by mere food. Is this what it would be like to accept a bribe?

After the meal was gone, we still had half a glass of beer each. It gave us an excuse to sit a while longer.

THE NEXT MORNING — one week from the day we arrived in Lusaka — we sat in our room at the hostel before going to purchase our train tickets. A dim glow filtering through the vine-covered window cast a gloomy light. The concrete floor between our two cots, was greasy and black.

"I want to get out of here," Gen said. "I hate this place." Her body trembled with feeling.

We got to the ticket office at the train station thirty minutes before it opened. At 8:30 a.m. the hallway already smelled of perspiration, cigarette smoke, and fried food. Crowds of people elbowed their way, trying to get to the front of the line. Whitewashed cement walls in the small corridor echoed with the chatter of a dozen languages.

The next train to Dar-es-Salaam was scheduled to leave tomorrow — Tuesday, and, one way or another, we wanted to be on it.

For over an hour the line inched its way up a narrow stairway. In the second-floor corridor the crush of people behind threatened to flatten us against the wall. Along the way, we fell into conversation with a British couple. The woman's backpack rested on the floor and she slid it along as the line moved forward.

"How do you like Lusaka?" The woman asked in a pleasant cockney.

"I can hardly wait to leave," Gen said. Her words came in a rush. "I want to get on with our trip. In Lusaka everything is so expensive. Our room is filthy. Nothing has gone right."

Immediately, Gen apologized for unloading. But she'd spoken the truth. It was the way she felt. How else could she have answered?

"You know tomorrow's train is sold out?" the woman said. At that moment, the line began to move and the woman bent to pick up her pack. She set it down on the concrete, six inches from where it had been. "Nothin' left.'Cept third class."

Third class, I knew, would be out of the question for a long train ride. I wouldn't even suggest it.

Then the woman said, "I hear they're sold out until next Tuesday. Week from tomorrow."

Either Gen didn't hear her or she couldn't believe it. She looked over at me and said, "Listen, I want to go to the window. I'll buy the tickets, okay?"

I recognized her tone of voice. It meant: *There can be no failure in this mission.* "Okay with me," I nodded. "I'll wait over there."

The line moved into the small room with the two ticket windows — two dark cages. Faces of the ticket sellers were barely visible, peering out at the impatient crowd. Gen was part of that crowd and being pressed forward.

When she was almost to the window, Gen bent her knees to gain leverage in order to resist the push of the crowd jostling behind her. She extended her arms, pressing both hands against the cement wall. At the wall, she squeezed a foot to her left, struggling to hold her ground and not lose her place in front of the ticket seller's cage.

Now, after being in line for an hour-and-a-half, she was at the window facing the clerk through the bars, the crowd still pushing at her back. Hands with money passed over her shoulder to wave at the teller. Gen leaned forward, straining to hear something the teller was saying. From where I stood, I tried unsuccessfully to read lips.

Then, through the din, I heard Gen's voice. "FINISHED? IS THAT WHAT YOU'RE SAYING? FINISHED? YOU MEAN FOR TUESDAY. THE TRAIN FOR TUESDAY IS SOLD OUT?"

The teller was a Zambian woman. I watched her lips and imagined her soft voice, her rich African accent, though I couldn't hear. But I saw her shaking her head. I saw her gesture with her hands as if she were erasing possibilities.

Gen's shoulders had been straining to push her way to the ticket cage, now her shoulders slumped visibly as she stood before the window. The teller was repeating something. This time I thought I could read her lips. "Tuesday next," she said, shaking her head. "That's the soonest."

Gen turned slowly from the window. She couldn't look at me. She pushed her way back across the crowded room to where I leaned on the wall. "I didn't buy the tickets," she said as if I hadn't witnessed the failed transaction; my mood shifted from passive to indignant.

"You didn't buy the tickets?" My voice began to rise in pitch — then I caught myself.

We stood quietly for a minute and looked at each other.

I felt a kind of calm descend, and after a minute, when I could finally speak, I said, "Let's walk over to the Pamodzi? We can have a nice lunch there. What do you say?"

**2001**

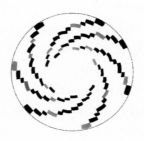

## On Safari

EIGHT YEARS AFTER we had served with the Peace Corps in Botswana, Gen and I were tourists just a few miles south of the border, in South Africa. During our time as Volunteers, we'd crossed into South Africa only to use the Johannesburg airport, but this week we were staying in Pretoria.

One morning, a van picked us up outside our budget-backpacker hostel at six-thirty. There were six of us in the van, two Brits, two Aussies, plus the two of us. A few minutes before noon, we were dropped off at the safari lodge near Kruger Park.

When we stumbled out of the vehicle we were greeted by a white woman in a red jacket with padded shoulders, black mini-skirt, and stiletto heels. Her style seemed almost bizarre — after all, we were "in the bush," as they say in South Africa, and we were bleary-eyed, hungry, leg-weary, and passive. Then she imposed a ceremony that reminded me of summer camp with a group of preteens — she said, "Hi, guys. I'm Wilma," and we lined up next to our van.

Introductions included the white-skinned owners of the safari lodge, Judy and Bruce, both of whom wore ranger outfits — khaki

short-sleeved shirts and short pants. As Wilma introduced them, Judy
and Bruce stood uncomfortably in front of our group, for the sake of
required ritual, and stared at us sleepily as if we had just interrupted
their nap. Bruce must have become paunchy over the years because
his uniform did not quite fit, buttons stretched dangerously over his
tummy. Judy was introduced as a wildlife biologist, though she seemed
ill at ease as if appearing in a stage costume. After the introductions,
Judy and Bruce disappeared.

Wilma spoke in a brassy voice as she walked down the row of
disoriented clients, her arm extended to shake each of our hands.
That done she said, "Follow me. I'll take you to the bar." Then with
an exaggerated wink, she pointed toward the lodge, "This way to the
bathroom." Her gesture implied that this was a little off-color secret.
The ceremony ended with assurances that the lodge staff was busily
preparing our lunch.

We had a few minutes to look around. According to the schedule,
we were only going to be at the lodge long enough to eat before being
packed into another van and taken further into the bush. Since I was
the only male in the vehicle I headed into the yard to stretch my legs
while Gen went to visit with the other women beside the pool.

A rockery formed a division between the driveway that lead to
the timbered lodge and the lawn. The large yard, with a green lawn
and a half a dozen small apple trees, spread to the north of where our
van had dropped us off. By my calendar it was May and springtime,
but in the southern hemisphere the season was late fall and the apples
had all been picked. On the far side three wart hogs rustled through
dry leaves. I watched them for a minute, and then walked around to
kill some time before lunch. I was wearing Birkenstock sandals and
the recently watered lawn cooled my toes as I walked under the trees.

Suddenly I was startled by a movement a foot away from my
big toe. A flash of black and a stirring in the grass. Something deep
inside my reptilian brain must have recognized danger and flashed
a warning. I froze.

At first, I couldn't see what it was and thought it might have been my imagination, but I moved my right foot and saw the motion again. A small black form curled around on itself and rose, spreading a hood below its thumb-sized head and revealing a pink mottled belly as it balanced, swaying from side to side. An immature cobra about a foot-and-a-half in length. In this part of the world cobras are able to spit their venom. They don't *have* to bite.

I stepped back and right away the snake appeared less aggressive. Its hood diminished in size, but it kept a wary serpent's eye on me. To my mind, that was okay. The creature was willing to have a conversation about this intrusion into his space rather than just biting my toe or spitting his venom. In that moment I couldn't even think about the consequences — blistered skin, blindness, bloated limb, poisonous attack on my nervous system, coma before death — but I felt relief and even a little bit of kinship with this fellow creature for having spared me my life. So far, at least.

Its forked tongue worked rapidly in and out. I took another step back. No need to get it riled up. When I retreated, it seemed to grow smaller until the green blades of grass swallowed it.

*Don't spit,* I said silently, putting more space between us.

After a pause of a few seconds he slithered off across the lawn toward the rockery. I wanted to make sure I knew where he was headed and took one step toward him. Immediately, he turned again to challenge me, raising up, spreading his hood to impress me that he meant business. Again, I backed off, then watched him move to the edge of the lawn, into a margin of black soil between the grass and the stones of the rockery.

I thought I ought to let someone know there was a poisonous snake in the yard. Expecting that Wilma would be working in the office and keeping my distance from the serpent, I walked up some stone steps in the middle of the rockery towards the lodge office.

The interior of the building was filled with artifacts to present a safari atmosphere — rustic over-stuffed furniture, trophies above the stone fireplace. But no one was in sight, everyone seemed to be in hiding. Then I saw Wilma in a cubicle, her red padded shoulders looming over the top of a desk near a computer.

A blue glow from the screen gave her face an eerie appearance.

"Hello," I said, alerting her to my presence.

"Oh, right," she said, and immediately snapped to. Her public relations training shifted into gear. When she turned and saw me standing before her in the office, I suddenly became "Client." She gave me her full attention, ready to answer any question.

I tried to keep my voice calm. "There's a cobra in the lawn outside." I wanted it to sound as if that might not be so unusual. There may be some circumstance that explained how this snake happened to be in the yard. I half expected her to tell me, "Oh that's Henry. Little Joey's pet."

Instead, Wilma deflected her eyes. She turned away as if she didn't want to hear what I had to say. "A snake?" she said. "I'm not too good with snakes." Then, to get rid of me, she said, "Wait outside a minute. I'll try to find somebody."

Talking with Wilma, I was very much aware that I was speaking to a recent graduate of a technical institute with a degree in hospitality and reception. Her pat phrases had the ring of familiarity. Her training could help her maintain control over matters of lodging, arrangements for food, or personal comfort, but faced with an event of nature — a cobra — she didn't have a clue.

Wilma wrung her hands and swiveled nervously in her chair, the spreadsheet behind her was frozen on the computer screen. "Someone will be right out." Visibly, she took a deep breath and moistened her lips with the tip of her tongue to collect herself. "Someone will take care of it right away."

I went back to the lawn where the snake still lay at the base of the rockery. Within a minute, an African man in blue overalls who had been raking leaves in front of the lodge walked slowly over to the top of the wall. His rake had been replaced by a six-foot pole, and leaning on the pole at the top of the wall, he looked cautiously over the rockery, letting his eyes adjust to the light. In contrast to the brilliant sunlight, he couldn't see the snake in the shade of the wall at first. I walked across the grass pointing to help him locate the serpent.

Behind him, a group of four African women came out of the kitchen talking loudly and laughing nervously. Two of the women ventured near the edge of the wall. With their arms folded across their chests, they leaned out, bracing themselves on a forward leg, ready to pull back. Below them, eight feet away in the soil, lay the small black cobra.

Within a few minutes, Judy, wearing her light-green khaki shorts, walked quickly out of the office. She had a yellow Walkman in her hand. A yellow cord ran from the device to a place under her blond hair. She looked vaguely annoyed, as if she had been listening to some music that she'd waited all day to hear and didn't want to be interrupted.

She saw me standing in the lawn and I thought I recognized the expression on her face. I had met several blond, blue-eyed people during my brief time in South Africa, and I'd found they weren't interested in anything I had to say. As soon as they learned I was an American, they didn't want to hear it. They'd heard it all. Ten years after the end of Apartheid, the way they saw it, their lives were in ruins. They were happy to give me a tour, serve a meal, or charge me for some other service. But when I started to talk, they moved away quickly, changed the subject, or went to sleep. Through their actions they were saying to me, just come, spend your money, and let us do what we do best. Then we want you to go home.

I pointed at the snake to help Judy locate it. Though I felt as if I was being helpful, I could see that she took the gesture as if I was giving her advice, telling her — "Here it is. Kill it."

Judy kept fumbling with her Walkman. There seemed to be a problem. The yellow earbuds fell down into her shirt.

*I could imagine that Wilma must have poked her head in Judy's office and told her the American had almost stepped on a cobra in the yard. At any rate, Judy must have heard a commotion in the yard. I had the impression that Judy might have been trying to catch up with her work during this time. The new safari group had just arrived and there was bookwork to do. Also, the staff had to get the food together. Get the van loaded. People are supposed to get fed then transported out to the camp in the bush. But things were not going the way they were supposed to. Guests were sitting around and when that happens they get bored, wander, and stir up trouble. And on top of it all there was this problem with her tape deck.*

The snake lay still in the dark cool soil. It looked small and black in the shadow.

*It crossed my mind that here were all these people inter-rupting their jobs to look for this snake. What if it wasn't a cobra? Maybe it was just a garden-variety, harmless reptile looking for lizards or small insects.*

The African man poked his pole into the dirt six feet away from it and the snake rose up, exposing its pink belly and spreading its hood. It looked the part of a baby serpent trying to be menacing.

"Stay back!" Judy said. "This is unusual. We don't get these things here normally." She said something to the women in the local language. Then she said to me, "Spitting cobra. Actually, Mozambique spitting cobra." She said something to the man with the pole. He smiled and stepped back from the wall. "We have a snake catching kit. And Steve is out on a trip today. But he's good with snakes. He'll take care of this when he returns."

*Steve?* I wondered about this "Steve" she talked about.

It was obvious that Judy wanted to establish control, to minimize the threat — and to not be bothered. It was important for her to be in control. The women from the kitchen stood behind Judy on a stone walk laughing nervously and making comments I couldn't understand, but Judy responded, speaking their local language in a rapid commanding voice. My guess was, she was telling them no one was to kill the snake.

Judy's manner and speech to her staff after I had gotten everybody excited with the cobra, seemed quaintly old fashioned, like someone trying very hard to reestablish old ground rules for a relationship that had been upset a long time ago. The women took her orders and admonitions with a grain of salt. They seemed to think about it before obeying or taking heed. There was a hesitation when they seemed to be sorting through their options.

Whites never directly addressed the problems between themselves and the Africans — in silence, tight-lipped, an attitude of soldiering on, the can-do attitude of a vanishing generation — but one certainly felt the tension and the undercurrents.

The nervousness of the women seemed to increase. They made jokes to one another making gestures showing where friends had gotten venom spit on them. One woman slapped her bare arms, apparently showing where blisters had appeared.

"What will you do then when Steve returns?" I asked. "Catch it? Take it somewhere else?"

"Yes. This is Africa, after all. We're in the bush." Judy was trying to adjust the pair of earbuds connected to her tape player. She seemed to be making one of them secure near her right ear. "Watch out. Keep your distance. If he spits he can hit me." She was standing at the top of the wall about eight feet away from the serpent. "He can spit a long way."

Her yellow tape deck went into the left pocket of her short pants. "*M'fezi* is what the Shangaan people call this snake."

"M'fezi? How do you spell that," I asked. "M-F-E-Zee-I?"

227

"No. M-F-E-*Zed*-I," Judy answered.

The snake moved toward the stone steps leading to the upper level of the yard and Judy moved toward the steps, as well.

"I just don't want it going into the lodge. Watch out!" Judy stamped her feet on the stone. The snake turned away. Speaking to the snake, she said, "Don't go into the lodge. Go!" She stamped her feet again on the hard surface and clapped her hands. The snake kept to the dirt border at the base of the rock wall. I followed it with my eyes as it crawled back about twenty feet, near the spot where I'd first seen it. Finally it disappeared into the wall where a boulder overhung and the concrete was cracked.

I wondered, if she could see the reality — this snake is dangerous. It's going to hang around. It'll be a danger to other safari clients later.

But Judy seemed averse to my presence and concern. Judy wanted everybody to buy into her illusion. She needed to assert control over guests and Africans. She wanted the blacks to believe in her power. She wanted me to believe in a mythical figure, Steve the Snake Man. But I couldn't believe that there was such a person here.

*Is it somebody on TV named Steve?* I saw a program once with a man named Steve who caught a mamba that had gotten into someone's house. Maybe Judy had seen the same show.

Just then Judy repeated, "We have the snake catching kit and Steve is very good with snakes. Gone today. But when he comes back we'll have him take this thing deeper into the bush."

# Glossary

*All non-English words in* Dusty Land *are Setswana, except as noted. Setswana is the language of the Tswana people of Botswana and other parts of southern Africa. It is written using the Latin alphabet.*

**A re a mmogo** [ă rē ă mō′·hō]    Follow me. Come with me.

**Aiyy** [ă ē′]    Exclamation

**Bakkie** [băk′·kē]    Small pick-up truck

**Baswara** [băs · wă′·ră]    San people

**Bata** [bă′·tă]    Tub for bathing

**Batswana** [băt ·swă′·nă]    People of Botswana

**Batswana pula** [băt ·swă′·nă pŏŏ·lă] (BWP)    Currency of Botswana (100 pula equals approximately $9.60USD as of 2017.)

**Biltong** [bēl ·tōng]    Jerky

**Bojobe** [bō·hō′bā]    Cornmeal porridge that accompanies every meal in Botswana

**Bua Setswana fela** [bu·ă Set ·swă′nă fĕ′lă]    Speak Setwana only.

**Bushveld** [bŭsh′vĕld]    A field or a plain of tall grass and low shrubs

**Combi** [cŏm·bē]    Modified VW van with seats for twenty passengers

**Corpulus** [cŏr·pŏ·lŏs]    A nonsense word from the author's dream

**Dipilisi** [dĭ·pĭ·lē′sē]    Pills

**Dumela** [dŭ·me′lă]   Hello.

**Farang** [fã·răng]   Foreigner (Thai)

**Ga ke bue Sekgoa** [hă kĕ bu′ā sĕkhō′ă]   I don't speak English.

**Ga pay [h**ă·p**ā]**   "Repeat yourself."

**Gape** [ha·pĕ]   Hello, again.

**Go siame** [hō sē·ă·mā]   Okay; very good

**Headmaster** (English)   In Botswana, comparable to the title "principal" as used in American elementary and secondary schools.

**Hum-bao**   A type of dumpling (Chinese)

**Ke klotse** [ke klōt·sā]   I feel satisfied. (Said after a big meal.)

**Ke na le nonyane mo offisi** [kĕ nă lĕ nōnyănĕ mo ōffēsē]   I have a bird in my office.

**Kgosi** [kgō′sē]   Chief of a village

**Kgotla** [kō′tlă]   The meeting place for a tribe; an important part of a system of conflict resolution; the offices of village administrators

**Koko** [kō′kō]   Word used in place of knocking on a door.

**Kraal** [k·răl]   A fenced space for goats or cattle

**Kwacha** [kwăsh′·hă]   Currency of Zambia

**Lolwapa** [lōl·wă′·pă]   A yard or a compound marked by a low wall where a family lives

**Makoa** [ma·ko′·a]   White man

**Mealies** [mĕ′·lēs]   See *Bojobe*

**'Mela** [me′·lă]   Shortened version of "dumela" (hello)

**M'fezi** [mm·fĕ′·zi′]   Mozambique spitting cobra (term used by the Shangaan people of South Africa)

**Mma** [mm · mă′]   An honorific referring to a woman, similar to "madam"

**Mmakadumo** [mm · mă · kă · dū′mo]   A giant snake

**Motswana** [mōt · swă′nă]   A citizen of Botswana

**N'goma** [n'gō · ma]   Witch doctor

**O ja dijo ga bedi?** [ō jă dējō hă bĕdē]   Are you eating for two?

**O rele** [o rĕ · lĕ]   You have something on your head.

**O tsogile jang** [ō tsō · gi′lā jăng]   How are you?

**Ocka** [ōck′ă]   Redneck (Australian term)

**O teng** [ō tĕng]   He/She is here.

**Paleche** [pă · lĕ · chā]   See *Bojobe*

**Principal**   Comparable to the title "president" as it used in American colleges

**Pula** [pŏŏ · lă]   See *Batswana pula*

**Rondevaal** [rōn · dĕ · vă′ăl]   A round house with a thatched roof (Afrikaans)

**Rra** [r · ră′]   Sir, mister

**Sala sentle** [să·lă sĕnt′lay]   Goodbye. (to those staying)

**San**   Bushman

**Setswana** [sĕt · swă′nă]   Language of the Tswana people

**Soi** [sō · ē]   Driveway (Thai)

**Tsamaya sentle** [tsă · mā′ă sĕnt′lā]   Goodbye. Travel well. (to those departing)

**Tswana** [tswă′nă]   Indigenous people of Botswana and elsewhere in Southern Africa

**Tuk-tuk** [tŭk·tŭk] Small, three-wheeled, motorized vehicle (Thai)

**Wa dzoha** [wă dzō′ hă]   Good morning (in xa tribal language of Botswana other than Tswana)

# Acknowledgments

I wish to thank my editor, Mary Beth Abel, for her persistence and staying power. She won't let things pass until they are absolutely covered in the text.

Thank you to Marian Haley Beil for her work in editing and design of the book, and rendering the graphic interpretations of Botswanan baskets designed and made by women of the Bayei and Hambukushu tribal groups that appear at the head of each story.

Thank you to my wife, Genevieve, for going along with me in joining the Peace Corps. She quit her career job to participate with me in this. But we had a wonderful adventure together in Africa.

A hearty thanks as well to all the people in Africa who contributed to the stories and to the book.

*In 2015, John Ashford published his first book about Botswana. In* MEETING THE MANTIS: SEARCHING FOR A MAN IN THE DESERT AND FINDING THE KALAHARI BUSHMEN *John tells of his life-long interest in the Kalahari Bushmen, and his and Gen's pursuit to connect with members of this storied indigenous African tribe.*

*The following excerpt is from the first chapter of* MEETING THE MANTIS.

■

## Chapter 1
### LOSING OUR WAY IN THE KALAHARI

On a bright, sunny day in Botswana, we made camp in a beautiful spot on the banks of the Okavango River. It felt like paradise on earth. Just a few yards from our tents the river curled and foamed under the lip of the bank. Several pairs of gray parrots called from the trees overhead and we heard the bark of baboons in the distance.

Gen and I hadn't been in Africa long and this was our first trip into the Kalahari Desert. It was our spring vacation from teaching and a few months after we had completed our Peace Corps training, and we were on our way to visit the San village in the Tsodilo Hills.

The drive to the Hills from our home in Tonota — across Botswana — was comparable to a trip across Texas. Because of the distance, the unpaved and poorly maintained roads, and our limited schedule, we would have only one day — tomorrow — for our visit in the village.

We were joined by two other teachers, Jim, who was British, and Marjorie, a Volunteer like us. All of us were novice travelers. We shared costs and traveled together in the cab of a small Toyota truck.

Following our arrival that afternoon we had made camp near a resort. In the evening, the four of us took a sunset cruise on the river, ate a sumptuous meal, and topped it all off with brandy. Returning to camp, everybody had a pleasant glow.

For the past several days Marjorie and Jim had been quarreling — and Gen and I were too often stuck in the middle of it — but that evening I noticed Jim and Marjorie crawl into the same tent. I hoped that the pleasant night had healed the rift.

The next morning I arose at sunrise and found a hippo wandering through our camp. I watched him until he ambled back into the river, then roused our friends so we could get an early start. After tea and a quick breakfast, we left camp knowing we could look forward to returning that evening to this garden of tall lush trees, wildlife, and colorful singing birds.

We drove until the road forked. There I got out of the cab and twisted the hubs of the front wheels to put the truck into four-wheel drive, because we were heading west along a narrow track of deep sand into an arid forest of stunted brown trees. The truck rocked slowly through potholes and ruts. Every mile or so our tires bogged down in the sand and we'd have to dig a wheel free. The metal of the truck was searing hot, and as we shoveled we had to be careful not to touch it. Inside the truck the heat was intense.

In the hope of generating a breeze, the windows were open, but along with the breeze came a swarm of small black flies. Gen, beside me, blew air through her lips.

"Phew," she said. "They keep getting in my mouth."

In the backseat, Marjorie beat the air vigorously with her hat to keep the insects away from her face. We were learning why the Kalahari was sometimes called "the land filled with flies."

Despite the discomfort, I was high with anticipation. We were on our way to meet a San group and see their rock art! The village was also an important place historically. Archeologists have found evidence that the village in the Tsodilo Hills has been in continuous use for at least 20,000 years, a time when the waters of a lake lapped against a nearby shore. In my mind, the San had lived there forever.

The truck's motion became hypnotic. The dry landscape made it easy for me to lose myself in my imagination. I imagined San hunters tracking antelope and small game. Under a wall of brush looming ahead, I half expected to see the naked legs of a hunter and his down-pointed bow, waiting for the movement of a desert hare. When the daydream receded, I saw only the tan burnt leaves of desert scrub, and although it was still morning, the sun was almost directly overhead.

As I drove, I remembered photographs and films I'd seen of San gatherers, women in skin aprons and shoulder bags, poking in the sandy earth with digging sticks, probing for tubers and edible roots. Those were the pictures in my naive mind, images of nomadic hunter-gatherers following a way of life as old as humankind. People in a land where resources were scarce who fostered habits of harmony and cooperation. I recalled seeing a film years earlier about Bushman hunters who killed a giraffe and then shared the meat among the entire band.

After two and a half hours, Jim asked from the backseat, "What're we looking for . . . I mean landmarks and such?"

"Limestone peaks?" Gen answered without much conviction. "Sticking up out of the desert?" The truth was, we weren't really sure, but none of us wanted to drive past and miss the goal of the entire trip.

The road narrowed even further and the truck continued its rocking, swaying motion. Occasionally the side mirrors knocked against thin trunks of scrub trees.

Four hours after leaving camp, the road circled the base of a large rock outcropping and we suddenly saw huts. We had arrived.

I stopped the truck when we came to a circular rail fence that enclosed a group of huts facing inward, some made of mud, and others of grass. Several large trees shaded the area. A dozen men and women, small in stature and olive-skinned, were clustered near the fence staring silently at our truck.

Three men walked toward us, hesitated and then began a conversation among themselves. They spoke in quiet tones, full of rustling sounds and clicks. They were Dzu Twasi, formerly known as the Kung and one of the many San groups in Botswana.

The San are considered by some anthropologists to be one of the most ancient populations in the world. Their language of clicks is very likely derived from the earliest forms of spoken language — the Mother Tongue. I knew about their language of clicks, but I'd never heard it spoken. I could not recognize any of their words, but as I listened it felt as though I was hearing the echoes of time. Hearing it spoken was like listening to a hunter step carefully over twigs or hearing the wind sweep across a field of grass.

Finally, one of the three moved toward me, gesturing as though to tell me something. He was barefoot and wore just a pair of khaki shorts with an animal skin in his a belt loop. He looked like the Bushmen I had seen in photographs. He spoke and gestured with his arms, but I didn't understand what he was trying to tell me.

Then I heard a voice say in English, "See headman."

For the first time I noticed a lean-to in the shadows about ten feet away. Inside two youths lay back braced on their elbows with their feet crossed. Then one of the young men sat up, leaned forward, pointed down the road, and called out, "Headman one kilometer. They saying you." After speaking, he returned to the universal posture of a teenage male. The only thing missing from the picture was a TV set.

I called to the men in my best Setswana, "We'll be back shortly." The man with the animal skin belt raised his hand to wave, acknowledging that he understood. I got back in the truck and started the engine.

Gen asked, "Where are we going?"

"To see the headman, I guess. Other than that, haven't a clue," I answered. "Down the road. We'll find out together."

We drove down the road about ten minutes until we reached a mud hut surrounded by corn stalks. Outside the hut sat a large man on a carved wooden stool. He had a corncob pipe sticking out from between his teeth. Definitely not a Bushman, his skin was a deep brown, almost black. He was solidly built with a broad chest. I guessed that he was a Humbukush tribesman.

I got out of the truck and extended my hand. Intuitively, I understood we had to pay this man although I was not clear about the reason. The arrangement seemed vaguely feudal. The large man rose from his stool and greeted me with a handshake. Of course, he knew what we had come for and looked happy to see us.

239

I greeted him in Setswana. "*Dumela.*"

"*Ehe, wa dzu.*"

"We want to see the rock art. The people sent us here."
I jerked my thumb in the direction of the village.

He started to say something, but was interrupted by a
coughing fit. Deep and rasping, the cough shook his body
in a violent spasm.

"Ten *pula*," he said when he recovered. He smiled,
but his eyes were dull and ringed with red. It was clear
that he was ill.

"Do I pay you?"

"Ehe." Yes.

I pulled two fives from my pocket.

He accepted the money, and then stuffing it in his
pocket, asked, "Aspirin? You have?" He patted the side of
his head. "Very hurt. Bad today."

Inside the truck, several pairs of hands rustled through
traveling bags. A bottle of Tylenol passed through the
open window.

"It's all I have," said Gen.

I shook out half a dozen tablets into the pink flesh of
the man's outstretched hand, and then, after checking in
the bottle to see how many were left, shook out a few more.

When we returned to the village, the three men were
squatting in the shade of a large mongongo tree near the
entrance to the compound. We all climbed out of the truck
and stood there while half a dozen women waved trinkets
for sale — bracelets and necklaces made from ostrich
shell beads. Whenever one of the three men tried to say
something to our group, the women shouted, drowning
out the men's voices.

The man with the animal skin belt introduced himself

as M'pao. He gestured toward the man next to him who wore a green sweatshirt. This man would be our guide. Then M'pao opened his hands in front of his chest, spreading ten fingers, making the gesture twice.

From the lean-to, the teenager who translated earlier called out, "Pay twenty!"

I peeled twenty pula from a ball of paper money in my pocket. The bill felt soggy with sweat. As soon as the women saw the money, they all screamed. When I handed the bill to the man in the sweatshirt, they screamed louder. They raised their arms, waved necklaces, and shook bracelets in the air. The screaming was not directed at me, however.

One woman, who was wearing a white blouse, red wrap skirt, and a blue cloth tied on her head, walked over to M'pao and began speaking angrily close to his face as she braced her knotted fists on her formidable hips. As her fists — still holding ostrich bead trinkets — pressed hard into the fabric of her skirt, the trinkets dangled at her side. There was a recognizable familiarity between the woman and M'pao that made me think they were married.

I gathered from her tone that she was upset about the distribution of wealth and that she spoke on behalf of the others as well. She finally backed off and rejoined her group. Watching this dissension, I asked myself, *Am I in the right place? Isn't this the culture that shares everything? That values harmony and balance between its members?*

These people were not fulfilling my long-held romantic notions instilled long ago in an anthropology class and reinforced by many books. What I was witnessing went against the grain of everything I'd ever learned about this culture.

Our guide, the man in the green sweatshirt, was named Selook. M'pao introduced us and I extended my hand eagerly. Selook's hand was limp. The top of his head reached the middle of my chest. I guessed he was about four feet eight inches in height. In addition to his sweatshirt, he wore shorts and a crumpled, tan golf hat. Selook might have been a suburban man ready to mow the lawn, except there was no lawn. His hat, with the rim pressed low on his brow, cast a dark shadow across his eyes and gave his deeply lined face an unhappy expression.

Without a gesture or a wave, Selook walked off toward a rock face. He led us up a trail through gray sand. His eyes were focused downward, his head hung down, and his hands were thrust into the pockets of his shorts. He looked like a man embarking on a grim task.

For a few minutes we followed a trail under a shelf of overhanging rock. Selook led us around the base of Female Hill, which is where much of the rock art is. He took us to view the well-known glyphs and pictographs of the Tsodilo Hills — described as the Louvre of Bushman art by Laurens van der Post and reproduced in books by him and other writers who have lived and worked with the Bushmen. Some of the rock art we were viewing could be thousands of years old. No one seemed to know for sure. All of the art I'd read about for so long was there: the lion with huge shoulders and mane and the eland antelope, with its chest swelling into a muscular triangle. There were trickster and shamanic images. There were many images of the hunt — Bushmen hunters with penises erect, showering arrows on a herd of unmoving antelope. All of the images represented some kind of power. In a shadowy rock niche, there were mysterious glyphs — oval shapes containing grids with dots and cross-hatchings. Questions about their meaning have kept scholars busy for years.

Selook guided us around the hillside to view the images on the rock, every image an icon, the hillside a temple. We followed Selook through this religious spot for two hours or so and forgot about the tensions among the people in the village. Instead, there was something almost narcissistic about the way we were caught up in our individual struggles for a better photograph.

At one point we walked a trail that wound past a boulder the size of a house and alongside a sloping rock wall. Walking under a stone overhang, we climbed the trail to a crack in the limestone. Then, rounding the base of the hill, we entered a grove of thorn trees where we marched in dappled light. A small Francolin hen — its face bright red and its plumage blending perfectly with the dry knee-high grass — scurried into bushes ahead of us. Remembering pictures of Bushman techniques for snaring ground birds, I tried to engage Selook in a sign language conversation. Gesturing, I acted out the snare, the bird walking into it, and the capture. I smiled as I made the signs.

A glint of sunlight on his hat made his expression look darker. His hands were still jammed into his pockets. A pained expression crossed his face as he stood politely, watching my gyrations. He let me finish and nodded to show he understood. Then his eyes shifted abruptly and Selook returned to the task at hand guiding us toward more indentations decorated by ancient hunters and walls scarred by the smoke of old campfires where a shaman may have led a trance dance.

As I followed behind him, I realized that this was his way of changing the subject. I suppose his clouded expression could be translated as, *Spare me! I have had enough of amateur anthropologists and would-be white Bushmen.*

Eventually the path circled back to the village where M'pao waited. He was squatting in the shade talking with another man who was wearing rumpled trousers and a dirty T-shirt. The other was standing awkwardly, as if he had been injured. His face was gray as dust. The puffiness around his eyes suggested a serious hangover. A few feet away, six women hunched down, feet flat on the sand, knees in the air. Everyone ignored us. It was a relief. There were low conversations in the clicking, rustling speech. A grandmother with a weathered face, the gold skin of her bare arms deeply seamed, chatted with a small child. Two younger women held souvenir strings of beads and laughed, sharing a joke. Everyone's tone of voice was subdued.

Quiet.

That was what I expected when we had first arrived hours earlier.

I wondered for a moment if the group was returning to a more traditional mode of behavior, but that thought was soon dispelled. At some signal of which I was not aware, the group made a decision to acknowledge our return and abruptly their behavior changed. The two women who had been chatting amiably suddenly began waving strings of white ostrich shell beads in our direction, each crowding the other for our attention.

Gen walked over to where the women displayed the jewelry, holding necklaces in their hands. She inspected several bracelets, letting the rough textured shells and seeds run through her fingers. Marjorie then aimed her camera at the group, but a woman shouted, indicating that Marjorie would have to pay if she wanted to take a photo. Marjorie let her camera dangle from a strap around her neck while she fished a five pula bill out of a small purse and gave it to the woman. Then another woman protested, Marjorie pulled out a five pula note for her. She aimed again and snapped her picture.

M'pao approached me.

"Show?" he said, holding up the palm of his hand toward me, as though he were a traffic policeman stopping traffic. I waited while he walked to a hut at the far edge of the circle. Then M'pao returned carrying a Bushman hunting kit with a three-foot bow and a quiver of arrows.

He held it up and pointed at his chest.

"You made it?" I asked. He nodded. "How much?" He gave me the same gesture he had made earlier when we arranged our guided tour.

"Twenty?" I asked.

The young men in the lean-to translated, we sealed the transaction, and M'pao gave me permission to take a photo. When the woman in the red skirt saw the money changing hands, she began shouting at M'pao again.

M'pao ignored her and slung the hunting kit over his shoulder. I focused my camera. Through the lens I watched M'pao puff up his chest and pull his stomach muscles tight. In the viewfinder he had the proud bearing of a hunter, while a few feet away the woman I assumed to be his wife shouted at him. His dignity seemed impervious to her attacks and M'pao remained perfectly photogenic. The woman disappeared into a hut before I finished taking my picture.

My attitudes had been shaken by the time we drove away from Tsodilo. Friction between the genders was obvious, but puzzling. I had always understood that decisions among the San people were made by consensus, and that the people shared among themselves. If so, why would the woman be so offended when Selook was chosen to lead a tour or that M'pao sold me a bow and arrow kit? I could understand if the wealth was being distributed unfairly — she was standing up for herself. But at the same time her anger seemed over the top. They seemed to be a group of people in crisis.

I wondered what had happened. Had an adviser come here and told these people that everything about their way of life was wrong? I could imagine a development worker or a consultant on tourism lecturing them: *It's a tough world out there. Forget about cooperation and sharing. For you to progress you have to learn to compete.*

There was something else I couldn't understand. Why did I have to pay the headman, a Humbukush tribesman? He was not San? It was an indication that the San were not regarded very highly — it was a feudal arrangement.

In the waning shadows of the day, we made our way to the main road. Back on this somewhat better maintained surface, the truck picked up speed. When I looked into the side view mirror I saw fine gray sand rolling off the tires and making a coil in the air behind, like a thread unraveling from a tightly wound spool.

■

JOHN ASHFORD grew up in Seattle, Washington and graduated from the University of Washington. After a lengthy career in teaching, and then as the director of a library, he began looking for a change. In 1990, he and his wife, Genevieve, went to Botswana with the Peace Corps where they both worked as teachers.

After returning to Seattle, John taught at Seattle Community College as a part-time instructor until retirement. His articles and stories have appeared in an anthology of Peace Corps writing, in *Silk Road Review*, in Seattle area newspapers, and other publications.